THE JOURNEY

VOLUME 2

LifeWay Press®
Nashville, Tennessee

DISCIPLES PATH

Disciples Path is a series of studies founded on Jesus' model of discipleship. Created by experienced disciple makers across the nation, it offers an intentional pathway for transformational discipleship and a way to help followers of Christ move from new disciples to mature disciple makers. Each study in the series is built on the principles of modeling, practicing, and multiplying:

- Leaders model the life of a biblical disciple.

- Disciples follow and practice from the leader.

- Disciples become disciple makers and multiply through the *Disciples Path*.

Each study in the series has been written and approved by disciple makers for small groups and one-on-one settings.

MINISTRY GRID®
training made simple

For helps on how to use *Disciples Path,* tips on how to better lead groups, or additional ideas for leading this study, visit: *ministrygrid.com/web/disciplespath*

Item: 005685160 • ISBN: 978-1-4300-3533-6

Eric Geiger
Vice President, LifeWay Resources

Philip Nation
Director of Content Development

Sam O'Neal, Joel Polk
Content Editors

Michael Kelley
Director, Groups Publishing

We believe that the Bible has God for its author; salvation for its end; and truth, without any mixture of error, for its matter and that all Scripture is totally true and trustworthy. To review LifeWay's doctrinal guideline, visit *lifeway.com/doctrinalguideline.*

Unless otherwise indicated, all Scripture quotations are taken from the Christian Standard Bible®, Copyright 2017 by Holman Bible Publishers. Used by permission. Scripture quotations marked (ESV) are from The Holy Bible, English Standard Version® (ESV®), copyright © 2001 by Crossway, a publishing ministry of Good News Publishers. Used by permission. All rights reserved. Scripture quotations marked (NASB) are taken from the New American Standard Bible®, Copyright © 1960, 1962, 1963, 1968, 1971, 1972, 1973, 1975, 1977, 1995 by The Lockman Foundation. Used by permission. (*www. lockman.org*) Scripture quotations marked (NIV) are taken from the Holy Bible, New International Version®, NIV®. Copyright 1973, 1978, 1984, 2011 by Biblica, Inc.® Used by permission of Zondervan. All rights reserved worldwide. *www.zondervan.com* The "NIV" and "New International Version" are trademarks registered in the United States Patent and Trademark Office by Biblica, Inc.® Scripture quotations marked (NLT) are taken from the Holy Bible, New Living Translation, copyright © 1996. Used by permission of Tyndale House Publishers, Inc., Wheaton, IL 60189 USA. All rights reserved.

To order additional copies of this resource, write to LifeWay Resources Customer Service; One LifeWay Plaza; Nashville, TN 37234-0113; fax 615.251.5933; call toll free 800.458.2772; order online at *lifeway.com;* email *orderentry@lifeway.com;* or visit the LifeWay Christian Store serving you.

Printed in the United States of America

Groups Ministry Publishing; LifeWay Resources
One LifeWay Plaza; Nashville, TN 37234-0152

CONTENTS

HOW TO USE THIS RESOURCE

Welcome to *Disciples Path: The Journey*. Over the course of one year you'll explore biblical stories of disciple-making and replication in order to gain a better understanding of what it means to follow Christ. As you get started, consider the following guides and suggestions for making the most of this experience.

GROUP DISCUSSION

Because the process of discipleship always involves at least two people—the leader and the disciple—each session of *Disciples Path: The Journey* includes a practical plan for group engagement and discussion.

This plan includes the following steps:

- **GET STARTED.** The first section of the group material helps you ease into the discussion by starting on common ground. You'll begin by reflecting on the previous session and your recent experiences as a disciple. After spending time in prayer, you'll find a practical illustration to help you launch into the main topic of the current session.

- **THE STORY.** While using *Disciples Path: The Journey*, you'll find opportunities to engage the Bible through both story and teaching. That's why the group time for each session features two main sections: **Know the Story** and **Unpack the Story. Know the Story** introduces a biblical text and includes follow-up questions for brief discussion. It's recommended that your group encounter the biblical text by reading it out loud. **Unpack the Story** includes practical teaching material and discussion questions—both designed to help you engage the truths contained in the biblical text. To make the most of your experience, use the provided material as a launching point for deeper conversation. As you read through the teaching material and engage the questions as a group, be thinking of how the truths you're exploring will impact your everyday life.

- **ENGAGE.** The group portion of each session ends with an activity designed to help you practice the biblical principles introduced in **Know the Story** and more fully explored in **Unpack the Story.** This part of the group time often appeals to different learning styles and will push you to engage the text at a personal level.

INDIVIDUAL DISCOVERY

Each session of *Disciples Path: The Journey* also includes content for individual use during the time between group gatherings. This content is divided into three categories:

Worship: features content for worship and devotion. These activities provide opportunities for you to connect with God in meaningful ways and deepen your relationship with Him.

Personal study: features content for personal study. These pages help you gain a deeper understanding of the truths and principles explored during the group discussion.

Application: features content for practical application. These suggestions help you take action based on the information you've learned and your encounters with God.

Note: Aside from the **Reading Plan,** the content provided in the Individual Discovery portion of each session should be considered optional. You'll get the most out of your personal study by working with your group leader to create a personalized discipleship plan using the **Weekly Activities** checklist included in each session.

ADDITIONAL SUGGESTIONS

- You'll be best prepared for each group discussion or mentoring conversation if you read the session material beforehand. A serious read will serve you most effectively, but skimming the **Get Started** and **The Story** sections will also be helpful if time is limited.

- The deeper you're willing to engage in the group discussions and individual discovery each session, the more you'll benefit from those experiences. Don't hold back, and don't be afraid to ask questions whenever necessary.

- As you explore the **Engage** portion of each session, you'll have the chance to practice different activities and spiritual disciplines. Take advantage of the chance to observe others during the group time—and to ask questions—so that you'll be prepared to incorporate these activities into your private spiritual life as well.

WHO IS JESUS?

Jesus is worth following because
there is no one like Him.

REFLECT

Welcome to Volume 2 of *Disciples Path: The Journey*. The goal of this resource is to help you explore the process of growing and maturing as a disciple of Jesus. Throughout the following pages, we'll examine the identity of Jesus as well as the identity and characteristics of a true disciple. We'll also explore what the Bible teaches on key issues such as God, humanity, the Person and work of Christ, the kingdom of God, the Holy Spirit, and the church.

In this session, we'll begin by gaining a better understanding of who Jesus is and why we should choose to follow Him.

What have you learned about Jesus over the course of your life?

Who do people say Jesus is today?

PRAY

Take a break from your discussion to approach God in prayer. Use the following guidelines as you connect with Him:

- Thank God for the opportunity to join with other disciples of Christ in order to gain a better understanding of who Jesus is.

- Praise God for the ways He has worked in your life and the things He has done.

- Ask for an open mind and heart to best see what He wants to reveal to you throughout this study.

INTRODUCTION

Jesus Christ. Most people have heard of Him. Most people have an opinion of Him. If you're looking for excitement, try going to a public area and asking people, "Who is Jesus?" You'll likely get a variety of answers and reactions.

The fact is, no one else has changed history and affected our culture more than Jesus. More books have been written about Him, more music composed for Him, more art reflecting Him, more architecture and buildings designed for Him, and more organizations and foundations created in His name than for any other person.

He changed history. In the name of Jesus, hospitals and orphanages have been built, the care for the elderly and homeless have been emphasized, and organizations for the hungry and needy have been created. Churches have been established in His name on every continent in the world. All this for a Man who never wrote a book, never attended a university, never ran for office, never led a company, and lived 2,000 years ago.

The question remains, who is Jesus?

Was He simply a Jewish carpenter turned preacher? Was He a political zealot? Was He a false teacher who deceived the people? Was He a misguided miracle worker? Was He a lunatic with a death wish? Was He a spiritual guru or teacher? Was He one among many or was He one of a kind? At the end of the day, everyone must answer the question, "Who is Jesus?"

In this session we're going to look at the uniqueness of Jesus. We are going to see what makes Him stand head and shoulders above the rest, and why He is worth following with all of your heart.

> *What is your reaction to the statement, "At the end of the day, everyone must answer the question, 'Who is Jesus?'"*

KNOW THE STORY

According to tradition, Jesus was 30 years old and living in Nazareth when He left His work as a craftsman and began His ministry. From this point forward, Jesus began to reveal His identity to a handful of men who would later turn the world upside down.

[35] The next day, John was standing with two of his disciples. [36] When he saw Jesus passing by, he said, "Look, the Lamb of God!" [37] The two disciples heard him say this and followed Jesus. [38] When Jesus turned and noticed them following him, he asked them, "What are you looking for?" They said to him, "Rabbi" (which means "Teacher"), "where are you staying?" [39] "Come and you'll see," he replied. So they went and saw where he was staying, and they stayed with him that day. It was about four in the afternoon. [40] Andrew, Simon Peter's brother, was one of the two who heard John and followed him. [41] He first found his own brother Simon and told him, "We have found the Messiah" (which is translated "the Christ"), [42] and he brought Simon to Jesus. When Jesus saw him, he said, "You are Simon, son of John. You will be called Cephas" (which is translated "Peter"). [43] The next day Jesus decided to leave for Galilee. He found Philip and told him, "Follow me." [44] Now Philip was from Bethsaida, the hometown of Andrew and Peter. [45] Philip found Nathanael and told him, "We have found the one Moses wrote about in the law (and so did the prophets): Jesus the son of Joseph, from Nazareth." [46] "Can anything good come out of Nazareth?" Nathanael asked him. "Come and see," Philip answered. [47] Then Jesus saw Nathanael coming toward him and said about him, "Here truly is an Israelite in whom there is no deceit." [48] "How do you know me?" Nathanael asked. "Before Philip called you, when you were under the fig tree, I saw you," Jesus answered. [49] "Rabbi," Nathanael replied, "You are the Son of God; you are the King of Israel!" [50] Jesus responded to him, "Do you believe because I told you I saw you under the fig tree? You will see greater things than this." [51] Then he said, "Truly I tell you, you will see heaven opened and the angels of God ascending and descending on the Son of Man."
JOHN 1:35-51

Notice all of the different names (or titles) given to Jesus. Why do you think there are so many?

Notice the two times the phrase "Come and [you'll] see" is used. What are people being invited to see?

UNPACK THE STORY

SON OF MAN

In this story, Jesus begins to reveal His identity to a few men. Each name or title for Jesus unveils an aspect of His identity as the God-Man.

Several of the titles attributed to Jesus in the first chapter of the Gospel of John reflect His humanity. "Rabbi" was a term of respect given to a spiritual teacher (see John 1:38). "Lamb of God" referred to His physical death on the cross as a substitute for our sin (see John 1:36). But the phrase "Son of Man" was special (see John 1:51)—it was Jesus' favorite way to refer to Himself. In fact, the Hebrew term is found 81 times in the New Testament Gospels, 30 of those in the Book of Matthew alone.

Why is it important to understand Jesus' humanity?

Jesus was a human, just like you and me. He wasn't a mythical person. He wasn't a legend. He wasn't an illusion that only appeared to be human. Jesus was a real, historical person.

The phrase "Son of Man" was a reference to His humanity. By using this term, He was declaring Himself to be a part of mankind. Jesus was a human, just like you and me. He wasn't a mythical person. He wasn't a legend. He wasn't an illusion that only appeared to be human. Jesus was a real, historical person. Hebrews 2:17 says that Jesus "had to be like his brothers and sisters in every way" so that He could help us in our time of need. John, one of Jesus' disciples, spoke of Jesus this way:

> We proclaim to you the one who existed from the beginning, whom we have heard and seen. We saw him with our own eyes and touched him with our own hands. He is the Word of life.
> 1 JOHN 1:1 (NLT)

John was saying, "We have heard Jesus, we have seen Him with our eyes, we have touched Him with our hands!" Jesus was fully human.

What questions or observations do you have about Jesus' humanity?

SON OF GOD

Another title given to Jesus was "Son of God." Nathanael declared, "You are the Son of God; you are the King of Israel!" (John 1:49). This term is a clear statement of Jesus' divine nature. While Jesus claimed to be fully human like you and me, He also claimed to be fully God, which is not like anyone else in human history.

Read the following conclusions from eyewitnesses to all that Jesus said and did.

- Peter—Acts 2:29-36
- John the Baptist—John 3:25-36
- John the Apostle—1 John 5:11-13
- Thomas—John 20:24-28

What are your observations from these passages?

What did the people closest to Jesus conclude about His identity?

Jesus wasn't just another moral teacher or spiritual leader. He was much more than that. Other religious leaders point to the way, but Jesus declared, "I am the way." Others claim to have some knowledge of truth, but Jesus said, "I am the truth." Others point to a path for living, but Jesus said, "I am the life" (see John 14:6). His claims set Him apart from everyone else.

Jesus claimed to be the "Son of Man"—fully human and the fulfillment of the promised Messiah. He also claimed to be the "Son of God"—God in the flesh who created the world, has authority over all things, and is coming again to judge and to rule. Ultimately Jesus backed up these claims by rising from the dead and showing Himself to be alive. The claims of Jesus are clear. But the response to His claims is a choice every person must ultimately make.

Jesus didn't leave us the option of labeling Him a good moral teacher. A good moral teacher doesn't claim to be God—unless it's true.

Was Jesus crazy when He made these claims? Was Jesus lying to the people around Him? Or was He who He actually claimed to be? One thing is sure, Jesus didn't leave us the option of labeling Him a good moral teacher. A good moral teacher doesn't claim to be God—unless it's true.

ENGAGE

Jesus is worth following because no one is like Him. He is completely unique. He stands in a class all His own. When we were far from God, estranged from Him and chasing our own way, Jesus came to us. But His coming wasn't celebrated with worship and obedience. His own people rejected Him. Yet to those who receive Him, to those who acknowledge Him and worship Him, He gives life. Consider how Paul states this in Philippians 2:5-11:

> ⁵ Adopt the same attitude as that of Christ Jesus, ⁶ who, existing in the form of God, did not consider equality with God as something to be exploited. ⁷ Instead he emptied himself by assuming the form of a servant, taking on the likeness of humanity. And when he had come as a man, ⁸ he humbled himself by becoming obedient to the point of death— even to death on a cross. ⁹ For this reason God highly exalted him and gave him the name that is above every name, ¹⁰ so that at the name of Jesus every knee will bow—in heaven and on earth and under the earth— ¹¹ and every tongue will confess that Jesus Christ is Lord, to the glory of God the Father.
> PHILIPPIANS 2:5-11

Why did Jesus become a man according to Philippians 2:5-11?

For those of you who can or would like to, take this opportunity to get on your knees for prayer. As you pray, acknowledge Jesus for who He is and what He has done. Commit your life to obeying and following Him. Pray for one another, that as a group you will worship and follow Him closely this week.

PRAYER REQUESTS:

....

....

....

....

....

....

In addition to studying God's Word, work with your group leader to create a plan for personal study, worship, and application between now and the next session. Select from the following optional activities to match your personal preferences and available time.

⬆ Worship

☑ Read your Bible. Complete the reading plan on page 14.

☐ Connect with God by engaging the devotional on page 15.

☐ Read Philippians 2:5-11 again. The conclusion of this passage states, "At the name of Jesus every knee will bow—in heaven and on earth and under the earth—and every tongue will confess that Jesus Christ is Lord." Begin each morning this week kneeling before Jesus. Worship and praise Him for who He is and what He has done in your life.

➡ ⬅ Personal Study

☐ Read and interact with "Jesus: Fully Human" on page 16.

☐ Read and interact with "Jesus: Fully God" on page 18.

⬅ ➡ Application

☐ Share with others. Take the time to share something you have learned this week. Maybe you can start at home with your family. Or maybe you know someone at work or in your neighborhood who has spiritual questions. You may also want to share your favorite verse with friends through social media.

☐ Memorize John 14:6: "Jesus told him, 'I am the way, the truth, and the life. No one comes to the Father except through me.'"

☐ Start a journal. Select one of the following passages and read it slowly several times. Consider what it's telling you about Jesus. Write down your thoughts and observations: John 1:1-14; 14:1-6; Colossians 1:15-20; Hebrews 1:1-4.

☐ Other:

 **WORSHIP**

READING PLAN

Read through the following Scripture passages this week. Use the space provided to record your thoughts and responses.

Day 1
Isaiah 9:1-7

Day 2
Isaiah 44:6-23

Day 3
John 6:22-33

Day 4
John 6:34-59

Day 5
John 8:12-29

Day 6
Romans 8:31-39

Day 7
Hebrews 2:5-18

WHO DO YOU SAY HE IS?

Before people can come to know Christ personally, they have to "come and see" who Jesus is. They have to do their own investigation. How did the prophecies of the Messiah point to Jesus? What does the evidence say about Jesus? Who did Jesus claim to be? What did others say about Jesus' identity?

Look at some of the following prophesies about the coming Messiah and how they were fulfilled in the life of Jesus. [Note: These prophecies were written in the Old Testament 500-1,000 years before the birth of Jesus.]

The place of His birth (Micah 5:2/Matthew 2:1)
The miracle of His birth (Isaiah 7:14/Matthew 1:18)
His triumphal entry (Zechariah 9:9/John 12:13-14)
Betrayed by a friend (Psalm 41:9/Mark 14:10)
His rejection (Isaiah 53:3/John 1:11)
His death with sinners (Isaiah 53:12/Matthew 27:38)
His hands and feet were pierced (Psalm 22:16/John 20:27)
He was mocked and ridiculed (Psalm 22:7-8/Luke 23:35)
Soldiers gambled for His clothes (Psalm 22:18/Luke 23:34)
No bones would be broken (Psalm 34:20/John 19:33)
A soldier pierced His side (Zechariah 12:10/ John 19:34)
He would be a sacrifice for sin (Isaiah 53:5-12/Romans 5:6-8)
His resurrection (Psalm 16:10/Acts 3:15)
His ascension (Psalm 68:18/Mark 16:19)

We started this session with the statement: At the end of the day, everyone must answer the question, "Who is Jesus?" Everything in this life and the next depends on how you answer that question.

Take some time to consider your personal conclusions about Jesus.

> *What stands out to you most about Jesus?*

> *What makes Him unique?*

> *What questions are you still wrestling with?*

> *Who do you say He is?*

JESUS: FULLY HUMAN

The term "Son of Man" identified Jesus as fully human. You may ask, "Why is this important? Wasn't it obvious that Jesus was human?" During the late second century, a group of people taught that Jesus wasn't fully human; He only "appeared" to be human. One of the early church leaders named Ignatius fought against that erroneous teaching. He wrote that Jesus "was really born, and ate, and drank, was really persecuted by Pontius Pilate, was really crucified and died … and really rose from the dead" (Ignatius, *Epistle to the Trallians*).

> **Look up the verses below and identify how Jesus' humanity is seen in each situation.**

> *John 4:6-7*

> *Luke 2:52*

> *John 11:33-35*

> *Matthew 4:1-2*

> *John 19:28-30*

You may also ask, "Of what relevance is it for me today that Jesus was fully human?" The answer is simple: Because Jesus experienced every range of human experience—pain and loss, anger and suffering, love and joy, hunger and thirst, temptation and disappointment—He can identify and sympathize with our hurts and weaknesses. Every emotion or experience you have gone through, Jesus has been through. And in your darkest moments you can turn to Him. He understands. He's been there.

Another reason Jesus used the term "Son of Man" for Himself was because this term was a prophetic title given to the Messiah. The Promised One would come from God, deliver people from their sins, and make them right with God. Look at the following prophecy about the coming of the Son of Man.

¹³ I continued watching in the night visions, and suddenly one like a son of man was coming with the clouds of heaven. He approached the Ancient of Days and was escorted before him. ¹⁴ He was given dominion, and glory, and a kingdom; so that those of every people, nation, and language should serve him. His dominion is an everlasting dominion that will not pass away, and his kingdom is one that will not be destroyed.
DANIEL 7:13-14

In this vision, how did Daniel describe the Son of Man?

Daniel saw the day coming when the Son of Man would be revealed as the Christ—the Messiah—the One who would bring the people back to God. And this was exactly who Jesus claimed to be. In John 1:41, Andrew found his brother and said, "'We have found the Messiah' (which is translated 'the Christ')." Nathanael declared Jesus as the "King of Israel" (John 1:49), another reference to Jesus as the Messiah.

Read the verses below. How did Jesus claim to be the Messiah?

John 4:25-26

Matthew 16:13-18

Matthew 26:63-64

What stands out to you most about Jesus' title as the "Son of Man"?

What is your reaction to Jesus' claim to be the Christ?

PERSONAL STUDY

JESUS: FULLY GOD

The Bible gives us several facts about Jesus that prove His divine nature.

First, Scripture tells us that Jesus existed before time. Jesus has always existed. Before time and space, before anything was created, Jesus existed. He existed eternally with God the Father, and through Jesus all things were created. In a confrontation with religious leaders, Jesus said, "You are from below ... I am from above. You are of this world; I am not of this world" (John 8:23). When they appealed to Abraham as their father, Jesus boldly declared, "Before Abraham was, I am" (John 8:58). In that statement He declared Himself to be God, existing before Abraham.

> *How does Colossians 1:15-20 describe Jesus' pre-existence and authority?*

Not only did Jesus exist before time and create all things, He chose to come into the world.

> ¹ In the beginning was the Word, and the Word was with God, and the Word was God. ² He was with God in the beginning. ³ All things were created through him, and apart from him not one thing was created that has been created. ⁴ In him was life, and that life was the light of men. ⁵ That light shines in the darkness, and yet the darkness did not overcome it. ...
>
> ⁹ The true light that gives light to everyone, was coming into the world. ¹⁰ He was in the world, and the world was created through him, and yet the world did not recognize him. ¹¹ He came to his own, and his own people did not receive him. ¹² But to all who did receive him, he gave them the right to be children of God, to those who believe in his name, ¹³ who were born, not of natural descent, or of the will of the flesh, or of the will of man, but of God. ¹⁴ The Word became flesh and dwelt among us. We observed his glory, the glory as the one and only Son from the Father, full of grace and truth.
> JOHN 1:1-5,9-14

> *What promise do we have in verse 12?*

Jesus also became a Man. Jesus came into this world, but He didn't come as a conquering king or a wealthy aristocrat. He came as a simple baby, born in a manger. He came in silence, on a clear night, in a small town in Israel called Bethlehem. He was born to common parents. Yet His birth was miraculous. God was becoming one of us.

> *Look at the birth accounts in Luke and Matthew. How did the angel describe this birth to Mary in Luke 1:26-37?*

> *Why is Jesus given the title "Immanuel" in Matthew 1:20-23?*

God came to us in the person of Jesus. He was in every way "God is with us." Jesus never ceased to be God, but He emptied Himself (see Phil. 2:7) and became a man so that He could die for our sin on the cross.

Jesus claimed to be God. While the Bible is full of statements about Jesus' identity as God, none are more powerful than the words of Jesus Himself. Take a moment to read Matthew 25:31-32; John 10:22-33; 14:6-7.

> *How would you summarize the claims Jesus made about Himself in these passages?*

Jesus demonstrated His divine power. Jesus not only claimed to have authority, but He also demonstrated His authority in many ways:

- Jesus demonstrated His authority over sickness (see Luke 4:40).
- Jesus demonstrated His authority over demons (see Luke 4:33-36).
- Jesus demonstrated His authority over sin (see Luke 5:20-25).
- Jesus demonstrated His authority over death (see John 11:43-44).

Ultimately, Jesus' greatest demonstration of His authority and the greatest vindication of His claim to be God was His own resurrection from the dead. Jesus told His disciples He would die and be raised to life again (see Matt. 16:21), Jesus was raised from the dead (see Matt. 28:1-10), Jesus showed Himself to His disciples after His resurrection (see Acts 1:1-3; 1 Cor. 15:3-8), and His disciples boldly proclaimed Jesus' resurrection (see Acts 2:29-32; 4:1-2).

WHAT DID JESUS DO?

Jesus is worth following because only

He can solve our deepest problem.

REFLECT

As we saw in the previous session, Jesus is both fully God and fully human—not 50 percent God and 50 percent human, but 100 percent for both categories. This unique identity reveals why Jesus is the only Being who could provide salvation for all people, and why it's critical for us to follow Him. Hopefully you had the opportunity to do additional study this week, reflect on the identity of Jesus, and even share what you learned.

Use the following questions to begin the session with discussion.

Which of the assignments did you explore this week? How did it go?

What did you learn or experience while reading the Bible?

What questions would you like to ask?

PRAY

Before moving as a group to the work of Jesus—including what He accomplished on our behalf—use the following guidelines to connect with God through prayer:

- Affirm your faith in the identity of Jesus as fully God and fully human.

- Affirm also your trust in Jesus as the Savior of the world and the Source of forgiveness for your transgressions, specifically.

- Pray that God's Spirit would bless you and the members of your group as you explore together Jesus' critical work in solving the problem of sin.

INTRODUCTION

In the late 1800s, scientists and doctors believed that diseases were created by "spontaneous generation." The idea was that diseases were random acts that popped up spontaneously from skin or the dust and could kill hundreds or even thousands of people.

Because these diseases were random, they couldn't be predicted or prevented. But a French scientist named Louis Pasteur boldly declared that the medical community had it all wrong. He claimed that there was an invisible world that couldn't be seen by the naked eye. This world was a world of micro-organisms. These micro-organisms could float through the air, attach themselves to food, be passed from person to person, or sit on contaminated objects and carry disease.

Immediately those who believed the research started washing their hands, separating the sick from the healthy, and covering their mouths when they coughed. But others scoffed at Pasteur's idea. The thought that there was an unseen world that was causing the problems of illness and death seemed strange. Today we know that Pasteur was right, and his groundbreaking research in "germ theory" paved the way for vaccines that have saved millions of lives.

In a similar way, the Bible tells us that we have an unseen problem. We see the effects of this problem every day. We live in a world full of crime, abuse, disease, promiscuity, rage, violence, and deceit. But while these things are bad in and of themselves, they're only symptoms of a deeper problem—a soul sickness. This soul sickness causes brokenness in our relationships on earth and brokenness in our relationship with the God of heaven. In this session we're going to discover that Jesus came to earth to solve our problem. He came to heal our soul sickness, to be the antidote that will restore people back to one another and back to God.

Where do you see evidence of "soul sickness" in today's culture? In your community?

What are some ways people try to solve this soul problem?

KNOW THE STORY

Nicodemus, a deeply religious man and member of Israel's highest ruling council, came to Jesus with questions on his mind. In this brief conversation, Jesus revealed the truth about who He is and why He came to earth.

2 ... "Rabbi, we know that you are a teacher who has come from God, for no one could perform these signs you do unless God were with him." 3 Jesus replied, "Truly I tell you, unless someone is born again, he cannot see the kingdom of God." 4 "How can anyone be born when he is old?" Nicodemus asked him. "Can he enter his mother's womb a second time and be born?" 5 Jesus answered, "Truly I tell you, unless someone is born of water and the Spirit, he cannot enter the kingdom of God. 6 Whatever is born of the flesh is flesh, and whatever is born of the Spirit is spirit. 7 Do not be amazed that I told you that you must be born again. 8 The wind blows where it pleases, and you hear its sound, but you don't know where it comes from or where it is going. So it is with everyone born of the Spirit." 9 "How can these things be?" asked Nicodemus. 10 "Are you a teacher of Israel and don't know these things?" Jesus replied. 11 "Truly I tell you, we speak what we know and we testify to what we have seen, but you do not accept our testimony. 12 If I have told you about earthly things and you don't believe, how will you believe if I tell you about heavenly things? 13 No one has ascended into heaven except the one who descended from heaven — the Son of Man. 14 "Just as Moses lifted up the snake in the wilderness, so the Son of Man must be lifted up, 15 so that everyone who believes in him may have eternal life. 16 For God loved the world in this way: He gave his one and only Son, so that everyone who believes in him will not perish but have eternal life. 17 For God did not send his Son into the world to condemn the world, but to save the world through him."
JOHN 3:2-17

What are some of the larger themes expressed in these verses?

What can we learn about Jesus from these verses?

UNPACK THE STORY

OUR PROBLEM

Jesus came to solve a problem, a spiritual problem. More specifically, *our* spiritual problem. But like many people today, Nicodemus was unaware that he had a problem. In his own estimation, he was a good, morally religious man. What could be his problem? But Jesus knew something that Nicodemus did not know. Jesus knew Nicodemus had a problem that was keeping him from knowing God deeply and personally.

Read the following passages. What is the problem? Who has this problem? What does this problem mean for us?

Romans 3:10-18,23

Ephesians 2:1

Romans 6:23

Like many people today, Nicodemus was unaware that he had a problem. In his own estimation, he was a good, morally religious man.

Nicodemus came to Jesus at night—in secret. He had questions for Jesus. He heard stories and wanted to know if Jesus was the real thing. And sometimes we may wonder the same thing. Does faith make sense? We may doubt. We're often uncertain.

When Jesus spoke to Nicodemus, He cut straight to the heart of the problem. With all his morality and religion, Nicodemus was a sinful man who desperately needed to start over. He was a man who needed to be changed from the inside out.

Describe the time when you first became aware of your own sinfulness.

GOD'S SOLUTION

When Jesus spoke with Nicodemus, He predicted His death on the cross when He said "the Son of Man must be lifted up" (John 3:14). This was God's solution to our problem. Jesus died as the full and final payment for our sin. Because the penalty of sin is death (see Rom. 6:23; Heb. 9:22), God chose to put our sin on Jesus to die as our substitute. On the cross, God poured out His wrath toward sin on Jesus, and He suffered in our place.

In what ways does the fact that Jesus took on your sin and died as your substitute affect your life?

Jesus told Nicodemus the reason for His death. Read His words again:

> For God loved the world in this way: He gave his one and only Son, so that everyone who believes in him will not perish but have eternal life.
> JOHN 3:16

Romans 5:8 says, "God proves his own love for us in that while we were still sinners, Christ died for us." Thinking about God's great love, the apostle Paul wrote these words:

> [38] For I am persuaded that neither death nor life, nor angels nor rulers, nor things present nor things to come, nor powers, [39] nor height nor depth, nor any other created thing will be able to separate us from the love of God that is in Christ Jesus our Lord.
> ROMANS 8:38-39

Romans 5:8 says, "God proves his own love for us in that while we were still sinners, Christ died for us."

Think about it. God sent Jesus, His only Son, to die in our place so that by His sacrifice we could be forgiven, restored, and made new again. And He did it all because He loves you. It was God's love that sent Jesus to earth. It was God's love that compelled Jesus to the cross. And it is God's love that draws us back to Him.

ENGAGE

During His conversation with Jesus, Nicodemus learned that it's not enough to be a good, moral, or even religious person. Everyone has a sin problem. And only Jesus can solve that problem. Jesus told Nicodemus, "You must be born again." When He said that He certainly didn't mean that a person must be born again in the literal sense. Jesus was speaking about a new birth. Just as a person is born physically, a person must also be born spiritually. When we turn from sin and turn to Jesus, we are born again. We can start over. We can become a new person (see 2 Cor. 5:17).

Spend time discussing what you've learned from the story of Jesus and Nicodemus and how it relates to your own story. Use the following questions as a guide for sharing your testimony.

What was your life like before you came to know Jesus?

Have you "passed from death to life" (John 5:24)? Be as specific as you can, sharing how you came to faith in Jesus.

Share briefly the difference Jesus has made in your life.

PRAYER REQUESTS

....
....
....
....
....
....
....
....
....
....
....

WEEKLY ACTIVITIES

In addition to studying God's Word, work with your group leader to create a plan for personal study, worship, and application between now and the next session. Select from the following optional activities to match your personal preferences and available time.

⬆ Worship

☑ Read your Bible. Complete the reading plan on page 28.

☐ Spend time with God by engaging the devotional experience on page 29.

☐ Connect with God each day. Every morning this week, commit several minutes to prayer. Ask God to help you solidify Jesus as central to your identity. Use the following prayer as a starting point. "Dear Father, because of Jesus, there is nothing I did yesterday that made You love me less and there is nothing I could do today to make You love me more."

➡ ⬅ Personal Study

☐ Read and interact with "Our Problem" on page 30.

☐ Read and interact with "God's Solution" on page 32.

⬅ ➡ Application

☐ Connect with your church. As an expression of the centrality of Jesus in your finances, give to your local church this week.

☐ Memorize Philippians 1:21: "For me, to live is Christ and to die is gain."

☐ Do something for someone. Find a practical way to help someone who cannot help you in return this week.

☐ Place Jesus at the center. Make a budget and a weekly schedule that reflects Jesus as central to your finances and to your usage of time.

☐ Other:

 **WORSHIP**

READING PLAN

Read through the following Scripture passages this week. Use the space provided to record your thoughts and responses.

Day 1
Psalm 34:1-22

Day 2
Isaiah 53:1-12

Day 3
John 10:1-21

Day 4
John 17:1-26

Day 5
2 Corinthians 5:1-21

Day 6
Ephesians 1:1-23

Day 7
Colossians 2:1-23

IN CHRIST ALONE

In 2002, songwriters Stuart Townend and Keith Getty sat down to collaborate on a new worship song. Getty proposed the tune that had a powerful and haunting sound, and Townend composed the lyrics that encompassed the themes of Jesus' life, death, and resurrection.

In an interview Townend said, "We've had some incredible e-mails about how people have been helped by the song through incredibly difficult circumstances."[1] One email came from an American soldier in Iraq who would pray the lyrics of this song every day and saw God's miraculous protection on the battlefield. The power of this song comes from the fact that its lyrics are rooted in the truth of God's Word.

Here are just a few of the lyrics from "In Christ Alone" that likely comforted the soldier in Iraq:

> What heights of love, what depths of peace,
> When fears are stilled, when strivings cease;
> My Comforter, my All in All;
> Here in the love of Christ I stand.[2]

If you haven't heard this song or want to be reminded of it's biblically-rooted lyrics, take a moment to search for the lyrics in their entirety on *hymnary.org*. Listen to the song or read over the words and ponder the hymn's rich meaning. This is a great way to worship Jesus and thank Him for all He has done for us.

Have you ever had a biblically-rooted song, book, or poem that has given you comfort during a difficult circumstance? If so, what was it and what made it comforting?

Take the time now to find a verse from Scripture or a line from a biblically-rooted song and write it down below. Spend time meditating on those words, and speak them aloud in a prayer to God.

1. Debra Akins, "Song Story: 'In Christ Alone,'" *Crosswalk.com* [online], 22 July 2004 [cited 14 October 2016]. Available from the Internet: *www.crosswalk.com*.
2. Keith Getty and Stuart Townend, "In Christ Alone," *The Worship Hymnal* (Nashville, TN: LifeWay Worship, 2008), 506.

OUR PROBLEM

The term *sin* was an archery term in ancient times. It simply means "to miss the mark." God created us to know Him, love Him, and honor Him in everything we do. But when we sin, we miss the mark of knowing, loving, and honoring God. Simply put, sin is anything that displeases God. When we break God's commands, ignore His teaching, rebel against His leadership, or put other things above Him in our lives, we sin against Him.

What questions do you have about sin?

At the core, sin is a heart issue. Someone once said that when you spell the word *sin*, the letter "I" is in the middle. And when I sin against God it's all about what I want, what I need, and what I desire. Pleasing myself takes the place of pleasing God. This sin problem beats in the heart of every person.

- Sin corrupts everything it touches.
- Sin destroys everything that's good.
- Sin perverts everything that's beautiful.
- Sin is at the core of every social and moral problem we face today.
- Sin is the reason we have prisons and rehab.
- Sin is behind every case of evil and injustice.
- Sin is the root cause of every addiction, enslavement, and abuse.
- Sin is why we suffer.
- Sin is why we feel alone.
- Sin is why we face sorrow, sickness, and death.
- Sin enslaves us and keeps us from God.

How do you see the effects of sin in our world today?

How have you experienced the effects of sin in your own life?

Much of the Bible addresses this sin problem and what it means for us. Read the following verses and journal your observations in the space provided.

I know, LORD, that a person's way of life is not his own; no one who walks determines his own steps.
JEREMIAH 10:23

Then after desire has conceived, it gives birth to sin, and when sin is fully grown, it gives birth to death.
JAMES 1:15

So it is sin to know the good and yet not do it.
JAMES 4:17

If we say, "We have no sin," we are deceiving ourselves, and the truth is not in us.
1 JOHN 1:8

GOD'S SOLUTION

The bad news of the Bible is that we have a sin problem. But the good news of the Bible is that God stepped in to solve our problem and to draw us back to Him. He did this by sending Jesus to us.

The New Testament tells us of Christ's coming in great detail—including why He came:

- **Matthew 1:21:** The angel Gabriel tells Mary about Jesus' mission in life.
- **Luke 19:10:** Jesus tells us His purpose in coming into the world.
- **Romans 5:8:** God demonstrates His love for us in Christ.
- **2 Corinthians 5:21:** Jesus came to be sin for us.
- **John 10:17-18:** Jesus went to the cross willingly.

We don't just see Jesus in the New Testament. Seven hundred years before the death of Jesus, the prophet Isaiah spoke about Jesus' death on the cross. Read Isaiah 53:4-6. As you read these verses, think about what Jesus endured on the cross for you.

> 4 Yet he himself bore our sicknesses,
> and he carried our pains;
> but we in turn regarded him stricken,
> struck down by God, and afflicted.
> 5 But he was pierced because of our rebellion,
> crushed because of our iniquities;
> punishment for our peace was on him,
> and we are healed by his wounds.
> 6 We all went astray like sheep;
> we all have turned to our own way;
> and the LORD has punished him
> for the iniquity of us all.
> ISAIAH 53:4-6

How does God's love demonstrated at the cross bring you reassurance and hope?

But Jesus' death on the cross isn't the full story. Jesus physically rose from the dead. And that is why Jesus is worth following, because no one else has done what He did. No one else paid our penalty for sin, dying on the cross and rising again from the dead.

Read the following passages and note how each points to God's solution to our sin through Christ's death on the cross.

John 5:24

Romans 10:9-10

Ephesians 2:8-10

2 Corinthians 5:17

Jesus stands head and shoulders above any other religious leader in history. All other religions in some capacity are based on the works and efforts of the individual. Salvation, forgiveness, and reconciliation are dependent on your performance—what you *do*. This includes the prayers you pray, the money you give, and the religious rituals you perform.

But Christianity is based on what has already been *done*. It's all about what Jesus has done for us!

In John 9:4, Jesus says, "We must do the works of him who sent me while it is day. Night is coming when no one can work." Then in John 19:30 Jesus declared on the cross, "It is finished." His work of reconciliation, satisfying the Father's justice against sin and opening up a way for people to be right with God, was finished. Any good works we do aren't to earn God's approval or to obtain forgiveness, but rather to express love and gratitude for all Jesus has done for us.

FOLLOWING JESUS

Jesus calls every person to follow Him.

REFLECT

In the last session, we looked at the work of Jesus and we discovered that He is worth following because He is the One who came to solve our deepest problem. Only Jesus died for our sin, rose from the dead, and offers life here and in the hereafter. These will be key themes as you move forward along your journey with *Disciples Path*.

Use the following questions to begin this session with discussion.

Which of the assignments did you explore this week? How did it go?

What did you learn or experience while reading the Bible?

What questions would you like to ask?

PRAY

Before you go further in this session, stop and pray together as a group. Use the following guidelines as you speak with the Lord together:

- Praise Jesus for all He has done for you.

- Ask Him to forgive you for any area of sin you have allowed to control your life this past week.

- Pray that you and the members of your group will gain a better understanding of what it means to follow Jesus in today's world.

INTRODUCTION

In 2006, the small upstart podcast company Odeo was struggling to stay alive. Just as it was about to launch a new product, Apple, Inc. came out with iTunes®, which included a robust podcast component. Odeo was dead before it even had a chance to truly live.

With only a handful of employees, the company's founder Noah Glass started day-long brainstorming sessions, trying to reinvent itself. In one session, Jack Dorsey, a web designer and one of the first employees of Odeo, had a new idea. Along with Glass, the two dreamed of a product that would allow a person to send a 140-character text message to multiple people at one time. Twitter® was born.

So how does it work? Twitter is an online presence for individuals and companies to easily send information—called "tweets"—to their followers. This information can be anything from a humorous quote to a link to an interesting blog to an advertisement for the latest product or service, as long as it's within the 140-character limit. A user is then able to control what information they see based on who they choose to follow. They are also able to encourage other users to follow them.[1]

Jesus' favorite invitation was simply, "Follow me." He invited people from all backgrounds, walks of life, and ages to be His followers. In just a few years, His followers were multiplying around the globe.

But following Jesus is different than being a "follower" on Twitter. Following Jesus changes everything—your life and your world. Today, we're going to learn what it really means to be a follower of Jesus Christ.

What comes to your mind when you hear someone say they are a follower of Jesus?

What do you think is required of a fully-devoted disciple of Jesus?

KNOW THE STORY

The global company known today as Twitter started with a few people who followed the vision and dream of its company founder. Within a few years, Twitter was a global player shaping our culture and the next generation.

In much the same way, the Christian movement had small beginnings. Jesus called a few people to drop what they were doing and sell out to His vision—and the rest is history.

> [18] As he was walking along the Sea of Galilee, he saw two brothers, Simon (who is called Peter), and his brother Andrew. They were casting a net into the sea—for they were fishermen. [19] "Follow me," he told them, "and I will make you fish for people." [20] Immediately they left their nets and followed him. [21] Going on from there, he saw two other brothers, James the son of Zebedee, and his brother John. They were in a boat with Zebedee their father, preparing their nets, and he called them. [22] Immediately they left the boat and their father and followed him.
> MATTHEW 4:18-22

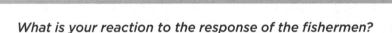

What is your reaction to the response of the fishermen?

What does their response tell you about them?

Are you still preparing your net or are you ready to leave the boat? Explain.

UNPACK THE STORY

A LINE IN THE SAND

Just reading this passage at face value, a person could easily think this was the first meeting Jesus had with these men. But it wasn't. The fact is Peter, Andrew, James, and John had been casual followers of Jesus for the past year and a half.

The Gospel of John fills in this gap between Matthew 4:17 and 4:18. We've already seen that Jesus first met Andrew, John, and Peter immediately following His temptation (see John 1:35-42). At that point, these men, along with Philip and Nathanael, began to follow Jesus. Think of them as Jesus' starting five! They went with Him to Cana where Jesus performed His first miracle, turning water to wine (see John 2:1-11). Afterwards, Jesus traveled with these men to Jerusalem to celebrate the Passover. There Jesus turned over the money changer tables (see John 2:13-17), encountered a Pharisee named Nicodemus (see John 3:1-21), and met a Samaritan woman by a well (see John 4:1-26).

But now after well over a year, Jesus was ready to call these men to a higher level of commitment.

Matthew 4:20, 22 state that "immediately they left" what they were doing and followed Jesus. Why do you think they felt such urgency?

Jesus was calling them to leave behind their old way of life and follow Him fully and completely. He was drawing a line in the sand and asking them to follow Him without reservation.

Up to this point, these men had been investigating the claims of Jesus. They had been learning His identity—He was fully God and fully man. Although they didn't comprehend it all, they were also growing in their understanding of the work Jesus came to do. But now Jesus was calling them to leave behind their old way of life and follow Him fully and completely. He was drawing a line in the sand and asking them to follow Him without reservation.

How have you responded to Jesus' call for commitment?

A DISCIPLE WHO MAKES DISCIPLES

From this point forward, Jesus began to prioritize His time with these new disciples. Just reading through the Bible we find Jesus with the crowd 17 times, but 46 times alone with His disciples.

It's clear that Jesus' strategy was not to *reach* the world, but to *train* disciples who would reach the world. Jesus' goal was not to *change* the world, but to *raise up* disciples who would change the world forever.

In what ways are you making yourself available to be raised up and trained?

A few chapters later, Jesus commissioned His disciples again saying:

> ³⁷ … "The harvest is abundant, but the workers are few.
> ³⁸ Therefore, pray to the Lord of the harvest to send out workers into his harvest."
> MATTHEW 9:37-38

As you work through this study, not only are you growing and learning how to become a disciple of Jesus, but you are also being trained to make disciples.

What's your biggest obstacle to becoming a disciple who makes other disciples?

Jesus' goal was not to *change* the world, but to *raise up* disciples who would change the world forever.

ENGAGE

The apostle Paul was a disciple of Jesus Christ. When he met Jesus on the road to Damascus, his life was radically changed. From that moment on, he was determined to know Jesus deeply and personally and to join Jesus in His mission to make disciples who make disciples.

Read aloud the following excerpt from Paul's letter to the church at Philippi. As a group, reflect on his words. Discuss how you can apply them to your own desire to know and follow Jesus.

> [7] But everything that was a gain to me, I have considered to be a loss because of Christ. [8] More than that, I also consider everything to be a loss in view of the surpassing value of knowing Christ Jesus my Lord. Because of him I have suffered the loss of all things and consider them as dung, so that I may gain Christ [9] and be found in him, not having a righteousness of my own from the law, but one that is through faith in Christ—the righteousness from God based on faith. [10] My goal is to know him and the power of his resurrection and the fellowship of his sufferings, being conformed to his death, [11] assuming that I will somehow reach the resurrection from among the dead. [12] Not that I have already reached the goal or am already perfect, but I make every effort to take hold of it because I also have been taken hold of by Christ Jesus. [13] Brothers and sisters, I do not consider myself to have taken hold of it. But one thing I do: Forgetting what is behind and reaching forward to what is ahead, [14] I pursue as my goal the prize promised by God's heavenly call in Christ Jesus.
> PHILIPPIANS 3:7-14

PRAYER REQUESTS

....

....

....

....

....

....

1. Nicholas Carlson "The Real History of Twitter," *Business Insider* [online], 13 April 2011 [accessed 14 October 2016]. Available from the Internet: *www.businessinsider.com*.

In addition to studying God's Word, work with your group leader to create a plan for personal study, worship, and application between now and the next session. Select from the following optional activities to match your personal preferences and available time.

⬆ Worship

☑ Read your Bible. Complete the reading plan on page 42.

☐ Connect with God by engaging the devotional on page 43.

☐ Talk with God each day this week. Every morning, commit several minutes to prayer. Ask God to help you understand what it looks like to be His disciple. Use the following prayer as a starting point: "Dear Jesus, allow me to recognize Your calling on my life and to respond with urgency. Release barriers in my life that prevent me from running after You. Continually grow me into a disciple that makes other disciples."

➡ ⬅ Personal Study

☐ Read and interact with "3 D's of a True Disciple" on page 44.

☐ Read and interact with "Fishing Lessons" on page 46.

⬅ ➡ Application

☐ Engage with others. Make a short list of people in your life with whom you think God wants you to engage. Pray that God will give you opportunities to invest in their lives by carrying out the principle of disciples making disciples.

☐ Memorize Matthew 4:19: "'Follow me,' [Jesus] told them, 'and I will make you fish for people.'"

☐ Spend time journaling. Write down your reflections on the following statements:
The moment I met Jesus my life was _____.
To follow Jesus and be His disciple will require me to _____.
I want to join Him in His mission, but I am often held back by _____.

☐ Other:

 **WORSHIP**

READING PLAN

Read through the following Scripture passages this week. Use the space provided to record your thoughts and responses.

Day 1
Mark 10:17-31

Day 2
Mark 16:14-20

Day 3
Luke 9:57-62

Day 4
Luke 10:25-37

Day 5
John 15:1-17

Day 6
Romans 10:1-18

Day 7
2 Timothy 2:1-26

A DECLARATION OF FAITH

The following letter was written by an African pastor from Zimbabwe. It was found in his desk after he was martyred for his faith in Jesus. Take time to read it and reflect on the meaning in this powerful declaration.

I'm part of the fellowship of the unashamed, I have the Holy Spirit power, the die has been cast, I have stepped over the line, the decision has been made: I'm a disciple of Jesus Christ. I won't look back, let up, slow down, back away, or be still.

My past is redeemed, my present makes sense, my future is secure. I'm finished and done with low living, sight walking, smooth knees, colorless dreams, tamed visions, worldly talking, cheap giving, and dwarfed goals.

I no longer need preeminence, prosperity, position, promotions, plaudits, or popularity. I do not have to be right, first, tops, recognized, praised, regarded, or rewarded. I now live by faith, lean in His presence, walk by patience, am uplifted by prayer, and I labor with power.

My face is set, my gait is fast, my goal is heaven, my road is narrow, my way is rough, my companions are few, my guide is reliable, my mission is clear. I won't give up, shut up, let up until I have stayed up, stored up, prayed up for the cause of Jesus Christ.

I must go till He comes, give till I drop, preach till everyone knows, work till He stops me, and when He comes for His own, He will have no trouble recognizing me because my banner will have been clear.[1]

Journal your observations from this letter below.

1. As quoted in Dave Earley and Rod Dempsey, *Disciple Making Is ... How to Live the Great Commission with Passion and Confidence* (Nashville, TN: B&H Publishing Group, 2013), 90.

PERSONAL STUDY

3 D'S OF A TRUE DISCIPLE

A 3-D object is fully formed. It's not a flat, one-dimensional image or even two-dimensional with only length and width. It's fully formed with length, width, and depth, and usually lifelike. Jesus never called for some kind of one-dimensional, shallow commitment or lip service. He was looking for fully devoted followers. So let's use three D's to define a true disciple of Jesus. A true disciple is:

1. Devoted to Jesus. Jesus said, "Follow me ... and I will make you fish for people" (Matt. 4:19). Jesus' favorite invitation was simply, "Follow me." He used it 24 times in the Gospels. Jesus called Peter, Andrew, James, and John to follow Him, and they dropped everything. He spoke those words to Matthew, the hated tax collector, and Matthew left everything to follow Jesus (see Mark 2:14). The same invitation was extended to Philip from Bethsaida, and he followed Jesus (see John 1:43). He spoke those words to casual observers who praised Him with their words but were unwilling to change their lifestyles (see Luke 9:59-62). He even spoke that invitation to a wealthy, young ruler who chose to hold onto his own money and power rather than follow Jesus (see Mark 10:21-22). Jesus invited everyone to follow Him. But what does it mean to "follow Jesus"? For starters, it means to be devoted to Jesus by placing your trust and faith in Him for salvation.

> *How do Matthew 4:17; Acts 2:36-41; and Ephesians 2:8-9 describe how a person becomes a follower of Jesus?*

2. Developing the attitudes and priorities of Jesus. Jesus saw the potential in these fishermen, but it would take time with Jesus to develop them into trained followers. Over the next two years, they would begin to develop the same attitudes and priories as Jesus.

Love for one another:
By this everyone will know that you are my disciples, if you love one another.
JOHN 13:35

Self denial, even death:
34 Calling the crowd along with his disciples, he said to them, "If anyone wants to follow after me, let him deny himself, take up his cross, and follow me. 35 For whoever wants to save his life will lose it, but whoever loses his life because of me and the gospel will save it."
MARK 8:34-35

Learning and living the Word of God:

³¹ … If you continue in my word, you really are my disciples. ³² You will know the truth, and the truth will set you free.

JOHN 8:31-32

Allegiance to Jesus above all other allegiances:

²⁵ Now great crowds were traveling with him. So he turned and said to them: ²⁶ "If anyone comes to me and does not hate his own father and mother, wife and children, brothers and sisters—yes, and even his own life—he cannot be my disciple. ²⁷ Whoever does not bear his own cross and come after me cannot be my disciple."

LUKE 14:25-27

Would you say that the character and priorities of Jesus are being reflected in your life? Why or why not?

3. Deployed to make disciples who make disciples. Jesus said, "Follow me … and I will make you fish for people" (Matt. 4:19). No longer were these men going to settle for just fishing; now they were going to fish for people. From this point forward they were going to be captivated by a greater vision of multiplying disciples and taking the message of Jesus across the globe. And this is the same vision Jesus cast to His disciples throughout all generations.

¹⁸ Jesus came near and said to them, "All authority has been given to me in heaven and on earth. ¹⁹ Go, therefore, and make disciples of all nations, baptizing them in the name of the Father and of the Son and of the Holy Spirit, ²⁰ teaching them to observe everything I have commanded you. And remember, I am with you always, to the end of the age."

MATTHEW 28:18-20

A disciple is a person who is devoted to Jesus, developing the character/priorities of Jesus, and deployed to make disciples who make disciples. A true disciple is devoted, developed, and deployed.

In what areas of life have you experienced consistent spiritual growth? In what areas do you still need to grow?

FISHING LESSONS

The word "disciple" is a term used for a follower of Jesus. It's an important word. It comes from the Greek word *mathetes* which means "a learner." In Jesus' day, a disciple was a person who followed a master to learn from him and to ultimately carry out his work. The Hebrew word *taladim* carried the same meaning—"a learner." It was often used to describe a scholar or rabbi in training. So "disciple" became the first word used to describe the followers of Jesus. It appears at least 230 times in the Gospels and 28 times in the Book of Acts. But what does a true disciple of Jesus look like?

In Luke 4:31–5:31 Jesus leads His disciples on six "fishing trips" to train them how to fish for people. Read and study each passage and write down what lessons the disciples are learning about "fishing." Notice who they are fishing for, what they do, and the final result.

Fishing Trip #1—Luke 4:31-37

Fishing Trip #2—Luke 4:38-44

Fishing Trip #3—Luke 5:1-11

Fishing Trip #4—Luke 5:12-16

Fishing Trip #5—Luke 5:17-26

Fishing Trip #6—Luke 5:27-32

What has God been teaching you about your own "fishing"? What is He instructing you to do? God has likely been taking you on your own fishing trip and has been equipping you with gospel nets to cast out. He is training you and teaching you concerning what it means to follow after Him.

How will you respond?

THE PRIORITIES OF A DISCIPLE

Following Jesus means living a life that reflects His character and priorities.

REFLECT

In the last session, we examined how Jesus invites people from all backgrounds, walks of life, and ages to be His followers. We also looked at how following Jesus changes everything—our lives and our world. We learned what it *really* means to be a follower of Jesus Christ. Hopefully you had the opportunity to do additional study this week and reflect on what you've learned.

Use the following questions to begin the session with discussion.

Which of the assignments did you explore this week? How did it go?

What did you learn or experience while reading the Bible?

What questions would you like to ask?

PRAY

Today we are going to talk about the priorities of a disciple of Jesus Christ. Before you continue into this session, stop and pray together as a group. Use the following guidelines as you speak with the Lord together:

- Seek after God with an open heart and mind to receive what He has for you today.

- Ask Him to reveal the priorities He wants you to have in your life.

- Pray that you and the members of your group will respond to the Holy Spirit's leading when those priorities are not in order.

INTRODUCTION

Shawn Klush is probably not a name you recognize. He was raised in a small coal-mining town in Pittston, Pennsylvania. Klush holds the title as the best Elvis impersonator in the world. In 2005, Klush became the grand champion at the World Elvis Tribute Artist Competition and was named the international champion of the BBC's World's Greatest Elvis Competition by more than 6.5 million viewers in the United Kingdom.

Currently Klush tours extensively, has produced three albums, and appears frequently in Las Vegas. Klush shared in an interview that he began imitating Elvis at the age of 2, but honed his imitating skills over time.[1] He says, "It's a natural thing for me to do. I say that with the utmost respect. It just comes very easy for me. I ran with it, not realizing it. Finally, after a long time, I realized, 'Wow, this is what I was supposed to do.'"[2]

Imitation is the greatest form of flattery, and true disciples of Jesus Christ are people who are committed to imitating Jesus. Over and over, Jesus told His followers to do what He did, live as He lived, and walk as He walked (see John 6:57; John 13:34; John 14:12; John 15:10; John 17:18; and John 20:21). Jesus said in Luke 6:40, "A disciple is not above his teacher, but everyone who is fully trained will be like his teacher." On another occasion Jesus said, "I have given you an example that you also should do just as I have done for you" (John 13:15). First John 2:6 says, "The one who says he remains in him should walk just as he walked."

All through Scripture we are told that God's plan for us is to be like Jesus. Romans 8:29 says God's plan is that we be "conformed to the image of his Son." The apostle Peter encouraged believers to follow in the steps of Jesus (see 1 Pet. 2:21). The apostle Paul said that he was going to keep working hard "until Christ is formed in you" (Gal. 4:19). And he told believers in Corinth, "Imitate me, as I also imitate Christ" (1 Cor. 11:1). God's plan for every Christ-follower is Christlikeness.

In what ways can a person imitate Jesus today?

What do you think is hardest about trying to live like Jesus?

KNOW THE STORY

Two years passed since Peter and Andrew first met Jesus. For the first year and a half, they followed Jesus at a distance, exploring His claims and coming to the conviction that Jesus was the Christ, the Son of God (see Matt. 16:16). Then they answered His call to "follow Him" and become fishers of people. During the next several months Peter, Andrew, James, and John shadowed Jesus, watching Him do miracles, heal the sick, cast out demons, and confront the religious establishment of the day. They were on a steep learning curve for sure!

But now Jesus was raising the stakes again. Two years into His ministry, the movement was growing so rapidly that Jesus needed to identify and train a few disciples who would lead the movement once He was gone. He spent all night in prayer, asking the Father for wisdom as He selected these disciples. Then He chose 12. Jesus would train these disciples for the next year and a half. Eventually, they would take the gospel to the ends of the earth.

13 Jesus went up the mountain and summoned those he wanted, and they came to him. 14 He appointed twelve, whom he also named apostles, to be with him, to send them out to preach, 15 and to have authority to drive out demons. 16 He appointed the Twelve: To Simon, he gave the name Peter; 17 and to James the son of Zebedee, and to his brother John, he gave the name "Boanerges" (that is, "Sons of Thunder"); 18 Andrew; Philip and Bartholomew; Matthew and Thomas; James the son of Alphaeus, and Thaddaeus; Simon the Zealot, 19 and Judas Iscariot, who also betrayed him.
MARK 3:13-19

Based on these verses, what qualities do you think Jesus was looking for in these disciples?

What does it mean to be "with" Jesus? To be sent out by Him?

UNPACK THE STORY

JESUS USES ORDINARY PEOPLE

Jesus hand-selected these disciples to be leaders. They were an interesting group to say the least. None were wealthy, highly educated, powerful, or from the ranks of the religious elite. In fact, the opposite is true. Most were hard-working laborers, others were political zealots, one was a dishonest tax collector, and still others were small-town nobodies.

Look at the way Acts 4:13 refers to Peter and John:

> When they observed the boldness of Peter and John and realized that they were uneducated and untrained men, they were amazed and recognized that they had been with Jesus.
> ACTS 4:13

These uneducated, common men were transformed by Jesus. That should bring us a lot of comfort. Jesus loves using common, ordinary people to do uncommon, extraordinary things!

Jesus loves using common, ordinary people to do uncommon, extraordinary things!

Being a follower of Christ doesn't mean we always do extraordinary things for God. What are some ordinary things a follower of Christ can do to advance the kingdom?

Jesus instilled His priorities and His character into His disciples. The end result was that they were fully trained to carry on the ministry Jesus began. Examine the following training experiences Jesus had with His disciples:

Matthew 11:2-19—How did Jesus train these disciples to deal with doubt?

Luke 7:36-50—How did Jesus train these disciples to exercise forgiveness?

JESUS DRAWS IN AND SENDS OUT

In Mark 3:14 we get a glimpse of Jesus' leadership training plan. Look at it again. Jesus called these disciples to be with Him and to send them out to preach. Jesus' leadership training plan was two-fold. First, He chose these disciples so they could "be with him." He wanted to draw them close to Himself, so they could learn in a deeper way about His power and authority over all things.

Describe a time in your past when you were mentored by someone.

Was this time beneficial to you? Explain.

Over the next six to nine months, Jesus taught the Twelve what it means to be a part of God's kingdom work. Jesus preached His two greatest sermons and taught repeatedly through parables and stories. He demonstrated His power over sickness, nature, and even the demonic. Jesus stretched their minds and exposed them to God's heart for the nations. But most of all, Jesus pulled these disciples close enough to see and embrace His priorities.

Second, Jesus sent the disciples out. He was preparing these disciples to go out and do what He was doing. It would be "on-the-job training," not just a classroom education. They got their hands dirty in ministry and eventually were released to go out on their own and do what He had trained them to do.

Read Matthew 10:5-23. Discuss your observations about this passage in terms of being sent out.

Jesus was preparing these disciples to go out and do what He was doing. ... They got their hands dirty in ministry and eventually were released to go out on their own and do what He had trained them to do.

ENGAGE

We have already seen that love is a priority of Jesus. Jesus taught us to love, especially those who can't repay or reward us.

> Pure and undefiled religion before God the Father is this: to look after orphans and widows in their distress and to keep oneself unstained from the world.
> JAMES 1:27

Take a moment to brainstorm how your group can practically demonstrate God's love to widows, orphans, and needy people in your community. Make some plans to put love into action.

Ways to demonstrate God's love:

To widows:

To orphans:

To those in need:

PRAYER REQUESTS

....

....

....

....

1. Accessed 13 May 2015. Available from the Internet: *www.shawnklush.com*.
2. Jeff Niesel, "King for a Day: Shawn Klush Reflects on a Lifetime of Imitating Elvis," *Cleveland Scene* [online], 8 January 2014 [accessed 30 April 2015]. Available from the Internet: *clevescene.com*.

In addition to studying God's Word, work with your group leader to create a plan for personal study, worship, and application between now and the next session. Select from the following optional activities to match your personal preferences and available time.

⬆ Worship

☑ Read your Bible. Complete the reading plan on page 56.

☐ Connect with God by engaging the devotional on page 57.

☐ Jesus had a habit of getting up early in the morning before daylight to pray. Experiment with this by waking up a few mornings this week before sunrise to worship God. You might choose some psalms to read or play worship music. Praise God for what He's done in your life. Ask Him to search your heart and reveal anything that's not pleasing to Him. Give Him your cares and concerns. Close your time by asking the Spirit to fill you and use you that day.

➡ ⬅ Personal Study

☐ Read and interact with "Jesus' Upward Priorities" on page 58.

☐ Read and interact with "Jesus' Outward Priorities" on page 60.

⬅ ➡ Application

☐ Spend some time journaling. Right on the heels of Jesus choosing His leaders, He preached one of His greatest sermons. The sermon is all about how to live like Jesus with a kingdom mindset. Take time this week to read through this sermon in Matthew 5–7. Write down your observations. What stands out to you? What questions were raised? What action do you feel God leading you to take as a result of reading this sermon?

☐ Reach out to a friend this week. Take him or her to lunch and share the priorities of Jesus you have learned. Talk about what priorities need to change in your life in order to begin to walk as Jesus walked.

☐ Memorize 1 John 2:6: "The one who says he remains in him should walk just as he walked."

☐ Other:

 # WORSHIP

READING PLAN

Read through the following Scripture passages this week. Use the space provided to record your thoughts and responses.

Day 1
Romans 8:1-30

Day 2
Romans 13:1-14

Day 3
Galatians 4:1-20

Day 4
Ephesians 4:1-16

Day 5
Ephesians 4:17-32

Day 6
1 Peter 2:11-25

Day 7
Colossians 3:1-17

GLASS VASE OF PRIORITIES

According to *Merriam-Webster's Collegiate Dictionary*, the definition of *priority* is "something requiring or meriting attention prior to competing alternatives." A priority is something that is *most* important. It's something that takes first place and is of greater value than anything else. When you look at the life of Jesus you will recognize that God's Word, prayer, obedience, love, and investing in others were the priorities of His life. Are these things your priorities?

A man was once given a glass vase, a bowl of pebbles, and a sack of large stones. He was told to put all the rocks into the glass vase. He started by filling the glass with the pebbles, but there was no room left for the stones. So he removed the pebbles, placed the large rocks in first, and then filled the gaps with the pebbles until they were all in the glass. The vase represents our lives and the capacity of time we have in a given day. We have many little "pebbles" that fill up our days: emails, deadlines, errands, favorite TV shows, or sporting events. If we aren't careful, our time can be filled with pebbles, and the big rocks are crowded out. But if we put the large stones in first—God's Word and prayer, love and obedience, investing in others—then the pebbles can fill the gaps and the big things in life won't get squeezed out.

>   *Which "small pebble" priorities are getting in the way of your*
>   *"large stone" priorities?*

>   *What do you consider the "large stone" priorities of your life?*

>   *What changes need to happen to make room for the "large stones"*
>   *in your daily routine?*

JESUS' UPWARD PRIORITIES

Part of following Jesus is developing the character and priorities of Jesus. The two personal studies for this week will dive into some of those priorities—both upward and outward. Carefully examine these priorities so you can replicate them in your own life. Use the passages under each priority as your guide.

First, Jesus made the Word of God a priority. Jesus saturated His heart and mind with Scriptures. At the age of 12, Jesus' parents found Him in the temple discussing Scriptures with the religious leaders. When Jesus was tempted, He resisted by quoting God's Word. Jesus often quoted and referred to biblical stories, never diminishing but always exalting the authority and validity of the Word.

> He answered, "It is written:
> Man must not live on bread alone
> but on every word that comes
> from the mouth of God."
> MATTHEW 4:4

In what ways have you used Scripture to protect yourself against temptation in the past?

> ³¹ Then Jesus said to the Jews who had believed him, "If you continue in my word, you really are my disciples. ³² You will know the truth, and the truth will set you free."
> JOHN 8:31-32

What does Jesus instruct us to do in this passage?

How have you experienced the truth setting you free?

Second, Jesus made prayer a priority. Jesus also lived His life saturated in prayer to His Father. When you look at Jesus' life, He prayed over every major event. He prayed at His baptism. He prayed as He chose the Twelve. He prayed during busy seasons of ministry. He prayed when He was grieving. He prayed when He was hurting. His last physical act on earth was to pray from the cross. And Jesus taught His disciples to pray as well.

> Very early in the morning, while it was still dark, he got up, went out, and made his way to a deserted place; and there he was praying.
> MARK 1:35
>
> Yet he often withdrew to deserted places and prayed.
> LUKE 5:16
>
> [39] He went out and made his way as usual to the Mount of Olives, and the disciples followed him. [40] When he reached the place, he told them, "Pray that you may not fall into temptation."
> LUKE 22:39-40

Jesus clearly had a pattern of prayer. Why do you think this was important?

Do you follow a certain pattern of prayer? If so, what is it?

We've looked at two key priorities of Jesus. As you reflect on these priorities, think of someone who you think models these priorities of Jesus.

How are these priorities lived out in a practical way in this person's life?

What can you do to implement these priorities into your life?

PERSONAL STUDY 2

JESUS' OUTWARD PRIORITIES

In the same way Jesus made the Word of God and prayer a priority, He also revealed upward priorities.

First, Jesus made obedience a priority. Jesus was always obedient to His Father. There was never a time when Jesus resisted or pulled aside from doing what His Father told Him to do. As a young boy, Jesus learned obedience to His parents. And as a grown man, Jesus lived a life of obedience to His Father, even when it meant suffering and death.

> [7] During his earthly life, he offered prayers and appeals with loud cries and tears to the one who was able to save him from death, and he was heard because of his reverence. [8] Although he was the Son, he learned obedience from what he suffered. [9] After he was perfected, he became the source of eternal salvation for all who obey him.
> HEBREWS 5:7-9

What do we learn about Jesus' obedience from this passage?

> [15] "If you love me, you will keep my commands." ... [21] "The one who has my commands and keeps them is the one who loves me. And the one who loves me will be loved by my Father. I also will love him and will reveal myself to him." ... [23] Jesus answered, "If anyone loves me, he will keep my word. My Father will love him, and we will come to him and make our home with him."
> JOHN 14:15,21,23

How would you like to respond to Jesus' words in this passage?

What is stopping you from responding that way?

Jesus also made love a priority. Jesus loved people in a deep and profound way. Jesus loved His parents. Jesus loved His disciples. Jesus loved the outcast and oppressed. Jesus even loved those who rejected and criticized Him. Jesus spoke often about the power and priority of love and compassion. Jesus also loved the Father and exalted the Father in everything.

[35] And one of them, an expert in the law, asked a question to test him: [36] "Teacher, which command in the law is the greatest?" [37] He said to him, "Love the Lord your God with all your heart, with all your soul, and with all your mind. [38] This is the greatest and most important command. [39] The second is like it: Love your neighbor as yourself. [40] All the Law and the Prophets depend on these two commands."
MATTHEW 22:35-40

What did Jesus say about the priority of love in this passage?

[9] God's love was revealed among us in this way: God sent his one and only Son into the world so that we might live through him. [10] Love consists in this: not that we loved God, but that he loved us and sent his Son to be the atoning sacrifice for our sins.
1 JOHN 4:9-10

What does Jesus' model of active love tell us about how we should love?

Finally, Jesus made investing in people a priority. Jesus drew large crowds, but His priority was training a few disciples who would change the world.

The next day Jesus decided to leave for Galilee. He found Philip and told him, "Follow me."
JOHN 1:43

Jesus sought out Philip and said "Follow me." In what other passages have you seen Jesus investing in people—making disciples that make disciples?

What one thing can you do this week to make people more of a priority in your life?

THE COST OF A DISCIPLE

Following Jesus will require sacrifice.

REFLECT

In the last session, we looked at the priorities of a disciple of Jesus. We had the opportunity to dig deeper into the priorities of Jesus and begin to apply those to our own lives. Take a few minutes to share something you learned this week or a struggle you are facing.

Use the following questions to begin the session with discussion.

Which of the assignments did you explore this week? How did it go?

What did you learn or experience while reading the Bible?

What questions would you like to ask?

PRAY

We have all experienced hardship, trials, and suffering. Today we are going to learn how to walk through those dark seasons by trusting Jesus completely. Before you dive into this session, stop and pray together as a group. Use the following guidelines as you speak with the Lord together:

- Praise God for the privilege of living as a disciple of Jesus.

- Ask God to make you aware of the sacrifices He will require from you as you follow Him in the weeks to come and beyond.

- Pray for the strength necessary to let go of anything and everything that hinders you from serving Christ and serving others.

INTRODUCTION

Dietrich Bonhoeffer is one of the world's foremost theologians and thinkers of the 20th century. He is most remembered for his courage to stand against the massive wave of evil that swept over his country. Bonhoeffer pastored churches in Germany during World War I and II and he saw the shifts within the German church under the pressure of the growing Nazi regime. As the German church officially supported the Aryan agenda, Bonhoeffer separated himself and led the establishment of a new "Confessing Church" that stood on the Scriptures. He left the safety of the United States to return to Germany during the most heated time in the war to join the resistance movement.

Bonhoeffer was hung in a concentration camp in Flossenburg just after his 39th birthday, but his legacy lives on in his writings. Dietrich Bonhoeffer was a man who understood more than most the cost of discipleship that he wrote about so convincingly. He was a Christian surrounded by suffering and yet he didn't hide from it—he embraced it with devotion to God and to the people he loved. Below are some of the greatest quotes from his book, *The Cost of Discipleship*:

> "To endure the cross is not a tragedy; it is the suffering which is the fruit of an exclusive allegiance to Jesus Christ."[1]

> "When Christ calls a man ... he bids him come and die."[2]

> "Costly grace is the treasure hidden in the field; for the sake of it a man will gladly go and sell all that he has. It is the pearl of great price to buy which the merchant will sell all his goods. It is the kingly rule of Christ, for whose sake a man will pluck out the eye which causes him to stumble; it is the call of Jesus Christ at which the disciple leaves his nets and follows him."[3]

Which of these quotes impacts you most? Why?

What are ways we can stand for Christ in our culture today?

KNOW THE STORY

Luke 9:51 says that Jesus "set his face to go to Jerusalem" (ESV). The phrase "set his face" could be translated "determined, resolute, steadfast." Jesus was focused on going up to Jerusalem. At this time He began to reveal to His disciples the death He would face there. Luke 9:22 says, "It is necessary that the Son of Man suffer many things and be rejected by the elders, chief priests, and scribes, be killed, and be raised the third day." This was the first of three clear predictions of His death, burial, and resurrection (see Matt. 16:21; Matt. 17:22-23; Matt. 20:18-19).

What awaited Jesus in Jerusalem was suffering and sacrifice. I'm sure the disciples were bewildered. They didn't fully understand what was ahead of them. Then Jesus turned to them and said these powerful words:

> 23 … Then he said to them all, "If anyone wants to follow after me, let him deny himself, take up his cross daily, and follow me. 24 For whoever wants to save his life will lose it, but whoever loses his life because of me will save it. 25 For what does it benefit someone if he gains the whole world, and yet loses or forfeits himself? 26 For whoever is ashamed of me and my words, the Son of Man will be ashamed of him when he comes in his glory and that of the Father and the holy angels."
> LUKE 9:23-26

Why do you think Jesus was calling His disciples to endurance?

What cost have you heard about followers of Jesus having to pay?

What price do you have to pay to be a follower of Jesus?

UNPACK THE STORY

FOUR TRUTHS

So far in this study we have seen the span of two and a half years of Jesus' journey with His disciples. He first called them to "come and … see" (John 1:39), to investigate His identity and His claims to be the Messiah. Then He called them to "follow me" (Matt. 4:19), promising to make them fishers of people. He invested the next six months showing them how to fish for people and make an eternal impact. He selected twelve emerging leaders, "whom he also named apostles, to be with him, to send them out to preach, and to have authority to drive out demons" (Mark 3:14-15). It was at this point He revealed His power and taught them what it means to be engaged in the kingdom of God.

At the end of this training, Jesus sent them out to the towns and villages to preach and minister to the people. The twelve apostles began to minister in Jesus' name, and God's power was on them. When they returned from their preaching tour, it was time for them to break away to rest and reflect. Jesus took them to the far north end of Israel, to a place called Caesarea Philippi. And it was there they talked about Jesus' identity as "Messiah, the Son of the living God" and His power to overcome evil (Matt. 16:16-18).

But at this point the mood changed. Jesus knew that His disciples had been fully trained. They understood His identity as the God-Man, and they were prepared to carry on the movement. Now His focus was on the cross. There are four important truths revealed in this passage:

1. We are not exempt. Many people feel that once they decide to follow Jesus they're promised a life free from trouble and trials, but that simply isn't true. Followers of Jesus face the normal hardships of life such as job loss, sickness, financial problems, pressures, and even death. All throughout Scripture we find suffering as a common and even expected occurrence in life. In 2 Timothy 2:3, Paul says: "Share in suffering as a good soldier of Christ Jesus."

What do you think Paul was trying to communicate in 2 Timothy 2:3?

2. We must deny ourselves. As Jesus moved toward the cross and His suffering, He called His disciples to deny themselves. "If anyone wants to follow after me, let him deny himself, take up his cross daily, and follow me" (Luke 9:23).

> Jesus knew that His disciples had been fully trained. They understood His identity as the God-Man, and they were prepared to carry on the movement. Now His focus was on the cross.

To deny yourself means to lay aside the things you desire and put Jesus first. It means to make Jesus the center of your life around which everything else revolves.

How will your lifestyle change if you deny yourself and put Jesus first?

What excuses keep you from following Jesus wholeheartedly?

3. We are to take up our cross daily. Jesus also called His disciples to sacrifice. After He told them to deny themselves He told them to take up their cross daily (see Luke 9:23). The cross was an instrument of Roman torture. It was a symbol of suffering and death. For His disciples to "take up his cross daily" meant their willingness to suffer for the name of Jesus, even if it meant death on a cross. Today Jesus calls us to follow Him, even when following Him may come at a high price.

> Whoever does not bear his own cross and come after me cannot be my disciple.
> LUKE 14:27

What emotions did you experience when you read these words?

4. We are called to follow Jesus. After challenging His disciples to deny themselves and take up their cross daily, Jesus simply said, "follow me" (Luke 9:23). Jesus was saying that a true follower endures. Even in the midst of hardship and trial, even in suffering and pain, those who are His are those who continue to follow Him.

What do you find most difficult about following Jesus in the middle of your suffering?

What is the reward for walking with Jesus through suffering?

To deny yourself means to lay aside the things you desire and put Jesus first. It means to make Jesus the center of your life around which everything else revolves.

ENGAGE

According to the Ethics and Religious Liberties Commission of the Southern Baptist Convention, "More Christians were martyred in the 20th century than in all previous centuries combined." According to statistics from Nigeria, India, and Iraq, it is estimated that currently more than 200 million Christians are being persecuted worldwide.

Many believers live in very dark and hostile places around the world and are extremely vulnerable to danger or even death. These believers are people like you and me. They have families, friends, and homes. They have worries and fears about the future. They want what's best for the ones they love. And they are choosing to follow Jesus in the face of great opposition.[4]

Take a moment to pray for our brothers and sisters around the world who are enduring suffering today. Ask God to give them mercy and grace to endure. Also, ask the Lord to give them boldness to share Christ in the middle of their suffering. Join with them in praying for a spiritual awakening in those closed nations.

PRAYER REQUESTS

....

....

....

....

....

....

....

....

....

....

1. Dietrich Bonhoeffer, *The Cost of Discipleship* (New York: SCM Press, Ltd., 1959), 88.
2. Ibid, 11.
3. Ibid, 45.
4. "Christian Persecution: Quick Facts: Reliable and Informative Snapshots of the Focus Issue," The Ethics and Religious Liberty Commission. Available at: *erlc.com*.

In addition to studying God's Word, work with your group leader to create a plan for personal study, worship, and application between now and the next session. Select from the following optional activities to match your personal preferences and available time.

↑ Worship

☑ Read your Bible. Complete the reading plan on page 70.

☐ Connect with God by engaging the devotional on page 71.

☐ Sometimes the greatest worship we offer the Lord is through our brokenness. Take time to be alone with the Lord this week. Read the story of a woman who worshiped Jesus through her brokenness—Luke 7:36-50. Cast your cares on Him—your worries, fears, dreams, pain, disappointments, and shame. Praise Jesus and anoint Him with your worship.

➡ ⬅ Personal Study

☐ Read and interact with "Four Truths" on page 72.

☐ Read and interact with "Put It Into Practice" on page 74.

⬅ ➡ Application

☐ Connect with others. Intentionally look around you for people who are hurting. Ask God to give you His eyes of compassion to see hurting people in your family, office, neighborhood, or school. Do something this week to demonstrate love and compassion to that hurting person. As you love him or her, Christ is loving that person through you.

☐ Memorize Luke 9:23: "If anyone wants to follow after me, let him deny himself, take up his cross daily, and follow me."

☐ Write an email this week and send it to someone who is going through a trial. Include in your email words of encouragement and promises from God's Word. Share how the Lord has carried you through a trial in your life.

☐ Other:

WORSHIP

READING PLAN

Read through the following Scripture passages this week. Use the space provided to record your thoughts and responses.

Day 1
Matthew 10:16-39

Day 2
Matthew 24:1-27

Day 3
Luke 14:25-35

Day 4
John 16:1-33

Day 5
Philippians 1:12-30

Day 6
Philippians 3:1-21

Day 7
2 Timothy 3:1-17

NO TURNING BACK

In the 1800s, a revival movement exploded across India. Hundreds of missionaries from Europe, Australia, and the United States flooded into the country, especially in the once closed territory of northern India. While resistance to the gospel was at times hostile and many missionaries were martyred for their faith, the gospel continued to spread rapidly. A Welsh missionary who had endured many persecutions for his faith led a family to Christ in the province of Assam. The tribal leaders decided to make an example of this family, forcing them to recant or be executed. Witnesses reported that when asked to recant or see his children murdered, the man simply replied, "I have decided to follow Jesus, and there is no turning back."

After the death of his children he reportedly said, "The world can be behind me, but the cross is still before me." And after seeing his wife shot with arrows, the man declared, "Though no one is here to go with me, still I will follow Jesus." After this statement of faith, the man joined his family in heaven.

The story of this man's courage spread rapidly and his entire village came to Christ, including those who carried out the senseless murders. Word of this man and the revival reached a famous Indian evangelist, Sadhu Singh, who put these dying words into a song that was sung all through the churches in India. This song was sung at many Billy Graham crusades and had a profound effect on thousands upon thousands of people. Reflect on the words of this song. Have you decided to follow Jesus no matter what?

> I have decided to follow Jesus;
> No turning back, no turning back.[5]

If you haven't heard this song or want to be reminded of it's biblically-rooted lyrics, take a moment to search for the lyrics in their entirety on *www.hymnary.org*. Listen to the song or read over the words and ponder the hymn's rich meaning. This is a great way to worship Jesus and thank Him for all He has done for us.

Take the time now to find a verse from Scripture or a line from a biblically-rooted song and write it down below. Spend time meditating on those words, and speak them aloud in a prayer to God.

5. John Clark, "I Have Decided to Follow Jesus," *The Baptist Hymnal* (Nashville, TN: Convention Press, 1991), 305.

FOUR TRUTHS

Go even deeper into the text this week as you study four primary truths found in Luke 9:23-26. Reread the passage and the "Unpack the Story" section to familiarize yourself with the text.

1. We are not exempt. Trials are part of life. They come to Christians and non-Christians alike. But in Christ we approach trials differently. Instead of being shocked or caught off guard by trials, we anticipate them, knowing that through Christ we can overcome any trial we face (see Rom. 8:37). In fact, as we see trials in our lives from God's perspective, we realize that every problem we face is another opportunity to trust God and mature as a follower of Jesus. Through them, God is producing in us patience, endurance, strength, character, hope, and faith. Just as weights in a gym break down muscles only to make them stronger, the struggles of life serve to make us stronger as we put our whole weight down on God's promises and trust Jesus to carry us through.

> ³ And not only that, but we also rejoice in our afflictions, because we know that affliction produces endurance, ⁴ endurance produces proven character, and proven character produces hope. ⁵ This hope will not disappoint us, because God's love has been poured out in our hearts through the Holy Spirit who was given to us.
> ROMANS 5:3-5

What do these verses tell us about the trials God allows to come into the life of every believer?

2. We must deny ourselves. Denying ourselves is a call to godly and holy living. When we deny our natural desire to sin in order to please God, then we are living a life that honors Christ.

Jesus encountered three men who wanted to follow Him, but each man had an excuse. Read this account in Luke 9:57-62 and answer the following questions.

In what way was each man unwilling to deny himself and follow Jesus?

What areas of your life would have to be put away for you to follow Jesus completely?

3. We are to take up our cross daily. Karen Watson was a missionary in Iraq. She was killed with four other missionaries on March 15, 2004. This is a portion of a letter she sent home to be read upon her death.

> Dear Pastor Phil & Pastor Roger,
>
> You should only be opening this letter in the event of [my] death. When God calls there are no regrets. I tried to share my heart with you as much as possible, my heart for the Nations. I wasn't called to a place. I was called to Him. To obey was my objective, to suffer was expected, His glory was my reward, His glory is my reward. ... I was called not to comfort or success but to obedience. Some of my favorite scriptures are: Isaiah 6, you know the one. 2 Cor. 5:15-21, 1 Peter 1:3, Col. 4:2-6, Romans 15:20, Psalm 25 and 27. You can look through my Scofield and see where it is marked. Please use only what you want or feel is best. There is no Joy outside of knowing Jesus and serving Him. I love you two and my church family.
>
> In His care,
> Salaam, Karen[6]

In what ways does Karen's example challenge you?

4. We are called to follow Jesus. Consider the benefits of following Christ in the midst of trial.

> [2] Consider it a great joy, my brothers and sisters, whenever you experience various trials, [3] because you know that the testing of your faith produces endurance. [4] And let endurance have its full effect, so that you may be mature and complete, lacking nothing.
> JAMES 1:2-4

Think of a person you know who has walked through suffering and hardship and continued to follow Jesus. What does his or her story teach you concerning what to do when persecuted?

---

6. Erin Curry, " 'Keep sending missionaries,' Karen Watson wrote in a letter," *Baptist Press* [online], 24 March 2004 [cited 14 October 2016]. Available from the Internet: *www.bpnews.net*.

PUT IT INTO PRACTICE

We have already seen that part of following Jesus is self-denial. Most of our time is taken up satisfying ourselves as quickly as possible with the things we want. In what ways have you practiced self-denial lately?

Think about ways you can deny yourself and exalt Jesus. Maybe you could deny your urge to be first and let someone else go ahead of you. You might deny the urge to eat and use your lunch break to fast and pray. You could even deny the urge to entertain yourself. Instead of watching TV or going to a movie, spend time visiting someone in the hospital.

Ask God to show you the areas in your life where He wants you to practice self-denial, and then record your thoughts in response to the following questions.

What message does our culture send about personal happiness?

How does this influence your thinking or distract you from denying yourself and exalting God?

What are your hardest urges to deny? How have you overcome these urges in the past?

List five practical ways you can demonstrate self-denial to others. These may be people you're close to or people you've never met before.

As you have worked through this session, you may be walking through a season of hardship and trial in your own life. During these times it's important to draw close to the Lord and lean wholly on His promises and presence. Below are some promises God gives to those going through trials. Study each one and write down the promise. Which stands out to you? Who can you share these promises with this week?

Psalm 34:18

Isaiah 43:1-2

1 Corinthians 10:13

2 Corinthians 1:3-4

2 Corinthians 12:8-9

Hebrews 13:5

James 1:12

SESSION 6

THE FRUIT OF A DISCIPLE

A follower of Jesus makes disciples
who make disciples.

REFLECT

Last session explored the cost of following Jesus. We saw that the Bible has a lot to say about suffering and how we face trials and hardships as followers of Jesus. We also had an opportunity to discover God's incredible promises for those who are walking through trials and suffering. Today we are going to look at the incredible privilege we have of joining Jesus in His global cause to make disciples who make disciples. If you ever wondered how God could use you in a powerful way to make a difference in this world, you're about to find out!

Use the following questions to begin the session with discussion.

Which of the assignments did you explore this week? How did it go?

What did you learn or experience while reading the Bible?

What questions would you like to ask?

PRAY

Before you dive into this session, stop and pray together as a group. Use the following guidelines as you speak with the Lord together:

- Thank God for the opportunity to study His Word and learn about Him.

- As you pray, submit yourself to God as His servant. Be intentional about expressing your desire to obey Him in all things, including the work of discipleship.

- Pray that God would begin to prepare you for a new discipleship opportunity that will benefit you and others.

INTRODUCTION

Would you rather have a penny a day doubled every day for a month or a million dollars in cash? Most people would probably grab the million without even questioning it. But you might be surprised at how quickly pennies can pile up!

Day 1	$0.01	Day 11	$10.24	Day 21	$10,485.76
Day 2	$0.02	Day 12	$20.48	Day 22	$20,971.52
Day 3	$0.04	Day 13	$40.96	Day 23	$41,943.04
Day 4	$0.08	Day 14	$81.92	Day 24	$83,886.08
Day 5	$0.16	Day 15	$163.84	Day 25	$167,772.16
Day 6	$0.32	Day 16	$327.68	Day 26	$335,544.32
Day 7	$0.64	Day 17	$655.36	Day 27	$671,088.64
Day 8	$1.28	Day 18	$1,310.72	Day 28	$1,342,177.28
Day 9	$2.56	Day 19	$2,621.44	Day 29	$2,684,354.56
Day 10	$5.12	Day 20	$5,242.88	Day 30	$5,368,709.12

By the end of one month, one penny has exploded to more than 5 million dollars. That's five times the million dollars originally offered! Why is it so much more? Multiplication. By doubling your pennies every day, you unleash a tidal wave of multiplication. Every banker and business leader understands the power of multiplication. Every hedge fund investor or financial planner understands the power of multiplication. And Jesus understood the power of multiplication, too.

Jesus trained His disciples to make disciples who would make disciples. Within 2 years, His twelve disciples filled Jerusalem with their teaching (see Acts 5:28). In 4 years, the churches were multiplying and growing throughout all Judea, Samaria, and Galilee (see Acts 9:31). Within 19 years, they "turned the world upside down" (Acts 17:6). And within 30 years, the gospel was bearing fruit and growing around the world (see Col. 1:6). Jesus' disciples unleashed a movement of multiplication that continues even today to sweep around the globe and reach every people group on the planet.

Why do you think the early disciples multiplied so rapidly?

What keeps believers and churches from multiplying today?

KNOW THE STORY

In a darkened room, with only a candle to light the table, Jesus gathered His disciples for one last meal and spoke plainly about His coming betrayal and death. These were Jesus' final words to the disciples in whom He had invested three and a half years of His life. After the meal, He led them out from the upper room, down the stone streets of Jerusalem, out the gate, across the Kidron Valley, and up the Mount of Olives. Along the way, they passed through a moonlit vineyard. Cradling a cluster of ripe grapes in His hands, Jesus spoke to them about how their lives could be used to create a movement that would change the world.

[1] "I am the true vine, and my Father is the gardener. [2] Every branch in me that does not produce fruit he removes, and he prunes every branch that produces fruit so that it will produce more fruit. [3] You are already clean because of the word I have spoken to you. [4] Remain in me, and I in you. Just as a branch is unable to produce fruit by itself unless it remains on the vine, neither can you unless you remain in me. [5] I am the vine; you are the branches. The one who remains in me and I in him produces much fruit, because you can do nothing without me. [6] If anyone does not remain in me, he is thrown aside like a branch and he withers. They gather them, throw them into the fire, and they are burned. [7] If you remain in me and my words remain in you, ask whatever you want and it will be done for you. [8] My Father is glorified by this: that you produce much fruit and prove to be my disciples. ...

[16] You did not choose me, but I chose you. I appointed you to go and produce fruit and that your fruit should remain, so that whatever you ask the Father in my name, he will give you."
JOHN 15:1-8,16

What does it mean to produce fruit as a disciple of Jesus?

How do you respond to Jesus' words in verse 16?

UNPACK THE STORY

MEASURING FRUITFULNESS

Jesus is teaching an important principle here about fruitfulness. When a person chooses to follow Jesus, God expects that person to begin to bear fruit that brings Him glory and proves to people watching that he or she truly belongs to Jesus. You may be asking, "What is spiritual fruit?" Look up the following verses to find the three ways fruitfulness can be measured in a believer's life.

Galatians 5:22-23
Spiritual fruit is measured by _____.

Philippians 1:11
Spiritual fruit is measured by _____.

Romans 1:13
Spiritual fruit is measured by _____.

1. Character Fruit. Galatians 5:22-23 describes character fruit this way: love, joy, peace, patience, kindness, goodness, faithfulness, gentleness, and self-control. When a person receives Christ by faith, the Spirit of God comes to live inside that person (see Eph. 1:13-14; 1 Cor. 6:19-20; Rom. 8:9). The Spirit goes to work transforming that person into the likeness of Jesus from the inside out. The longer you walk with Christ, the more you are transformed by the Spirit to look more and more like Him.

> We all, with unveiled faces, are looking as in a mirror at the glory of the Lord and are being transformed into the same image from glory to glory; this is from the Lord who is the Spirit.
> 2 CORINTHIANS 3:18

2. Conduct Fruit. Another fruit in the life of every Christ-follower is conduct fruit. In Philippians 1:11, the apostle Paul speaks about the "fruit of righteousness." This is the fruit of a life that lives righteously and serves God faithfully.

Jesus is teaching an important principle here about fruitfulness. When a person chooses to follow Jesus, God expects that person to begin to bear fruit that brings Him glory and proves to people watching that he or she truly belongs to Jesus.

Followers of Jesus are called to be different from everyone else. Followers of Jesus produce good works (see Eph. 2:10; Titus 3:14) that glorify God and demonstrate His love to the world (see Matt. 5:16). So when you love God and love people, choose integrity and honesty, lead with compassion, serve with humility, and give generously, you are reflecting Jesus to the people around you.

3. Conversion Fruit. The final fruit in the life of a follower of Jesus is conversion fruit. The apostle Paul, in writing to the Romans, looked forward to a "fruitful ministry" when he arrived in Rome (see Rom. 1:13). He saw the salvation of many people like a huge reaping harvest at the end of a long season.

Jesus often used the same analogy. He spoke of people coming to faith as the reaping of a spiritual harvest. Jesus said, "The harvest is abundant, but the workers are few" (Matt. 9:37; see also Luke 10:2 and John 4:35-38).

When you share the gospel with a person far from God and they come to faith in Jesus, you are bearing spiritual fruit (see Prov. 11:30). When you invest in a person—just as Jesus invested in His disciples—and you teach him or her to walk with God and invest in others, you are producing lasting spiritual fruit.

Which area do you think needs the most attention in your life?

In which area are you seeing growth?

Who are you looking forward to investing in spiritually?

When you invest in a person—just as Jesus invested in His disciples— and you teach him or her to walk with God and invest in others, you are producing lasting spiritual fruit.

ENGAGE

In John 15, Jesus teaches us about bearing spiritual fruit. While Jesus could have been talking about character fruit or conduct fruit, most likely Jesus had conversion fruit in mind. He was casting a vision of what a fruitful life that makes disciples who make disciples looks like. This was the last time Jesus spoke to His disciples before His crucifixion and resurrection. For three and half years He poured His life into them, teaching them how to preach the gospel, minister to the hurting, and make disciples who make disciples. The original twelve were now becoming more and more like Jesus.

Now the Twelve had grown into 70 disciple-makers (see Luke 10:1). They were already beginning to multiply! Jesus envisioned a day when His disciples would multiply, making disciples who would make disciples, and their influence would change the world. But on this night, He used a simple object lesson of a vine, a branch, and some fruit to demonstrate His desire for them to multiply.

What things do you need to work on to live a more fruitful life?

Share some action steps you plan to take this week.

Disciple-making is a decision. No one will make you invest in others. It's a choice you make based on the command of Jesus (see Matt. 28:18-20). To get started, ask the Lord to give you the names of a few people you can invest in. Write the names below. As a group, pray over these names and how God will use you to share the fruit that God has brought to your life.

Names of people you plan to invest in:

PRAYER REQUESTS

....

....

....

....

....

In addition to studying God's Word, work with your group leader to create a plan for personal study, worship, and application between now and the next session. Select from the following optional activities to match your personal preferences and available time.

⬆ Worship

☑ Read your Bible. Complete the reading plan on page 84.

☐ Connect with God by engaging the devotional on page 85.

☐ Read 1 Corinthians 3:10-15 and 1 Thessalonians 2:19. What is Paul's source of joy when he stands before the Lord? Evaluate the way you spend your time, talents, resources, and relationships. Spend time before the Lord praising Him for His grace in your life.

➡ ⬅ Personal Study

☐ Read and interact with "Stages of Fruitfulness" on page 86

☐ Read and interact with "The Fruitful Life" on page 88.

⬅ ➡ Application

☐ Connect with others. Take someone out to lunch this week who doesn't know Jesus. Find out about him or her—background, struggles, stressors. Make it your goal in the next 30 days to begin to encourage this person in one area of his or her life. All the while, pray for an opportunity to share what Jesus has done for you.

☐ Memorize John 15:8: "My Father is glorified by this: that you produce much fruit and prove to be my disciples."

☐ Spend time journaling. In 2 Timothy 2:2 Paul mentions a four-generation movement of multiplication: Paul, Timothy, faithful men, and others. Once a person makes disciples to the fourth generation, a movement is born. Journal your own personal movement of multiplication. Who is your Paul (someone who has discipled you or invested in your life)? Who are your "faithful men" (those you could personally disciple)? Who are the "others" that your disciples could train?

☐ Other:

WORSHIP

READING PLAN

Read through the following Scripture passages this week. Use the space provided to record your thoughts and responses.

Day 1
Luke 6:27-49

Day 2
John 13:1-20

Day 3
Romans 15:1-21

Day 4
1 Corinthians 12:1-31

Day 5
Ephesians 5:1-21

Day 6
Philippians 2:1-18

Day 7
1 John 5:1-21

LASTING FRUIT

Mount Arbel is the highest point along the Sea of Galilee. On a clear day, from Mount Arbel you can see Mount Hermon that borders Syria, the Golan Heights that border Syria and Jordan, and Mount Carmel that borders Lebanon. You can also see the Via Maris (Way of the Sea) which was the popular trade route in Jesus' day that ran through Galilee and led travelers to the most powerful nations of the Middle East. From Mount Arbel you can see the world.

It's possible that it was here Jesus met His disciples one more time. The last time He had spoken to them about creating a movement of multiplication, they were together in the moonlit vineyard the night He was arrested. At that time He spoke to them about vines, branches, and fruit. But this time, He stood in broad daylight with His disciples in His resurrected body and looked at the nations. And He spoke to them words that would change them forever:

> [19] Go, therefore, and make disciples of all nations, baptizing them in the name of the Father and of the Son and of the Holy Spirit, [20] teaching them to observe everything I have commanded you. And remember, I am with you always, to the end of the age.
> MATTHEW 28:19-20

They had been trained. They knew how to lead people to Christ, and they knew how to invest in a few. And in a few days, Jesus would send the Spirit to empower them to ignite a movement that would change the world (Acts 2:1-41). They had everything they needed, but they still had to choose. They had to choose to follow Jesus, to live as He lived, and to walk as He walked.

The same thing could be said about us. We have the same Spirit they had. We have the same Word of God they had. We have the same command they had—"Go … and make disciples." The question remains, will we follow Jesus? The world is waiting for men and women who will dare to follow Jesus and join Him in His global cause to make disciples of all nations.

There is no greater joy or thrill, no greater reward or satisfaction, than joining Jesus in the greatest cause on earth! And when your life is over, you'll have lasting fruit to show for your life. Fruit that will remain forever!

What is your reaction to this passage in Matthew 28?

How will you join Jesus in His global cause to make disciples of all nations?

STAGES OF FRUITFULNESS

Take a moment to read John 15:1-8,16 again. As you read this passage, notice that Jesus refers to different stages of fruitfulness. See if you can identify them.

No Fruit: There are those who have no fruit (v. 2). These are the people who know Christ but have never invested in anyone spiritually. They have never trained anyone how to walk with God. Jesus said, "Every branch in me that does not bear fruit he takes away" (John 15:2, ESV). The phrase "takes away" literally means to "lift up, or to move somewhere else." Some translate it "to cut off." The idea is a branch that has fallen off the trellis and is in the mud. It's dirty; it can't get sunlight; and it can't get air, so it is barren.

There are many Christians like that. They have fallen into some area of sin or disobedience. They have become entangled in a quagmire of habits and behaviors that have grieved God's Spirit (see Eph. 4:30), and consequently they have nothing to show for their walk with Christ. But here's the good news: Even if you have fallen and you aren't bearing fruit for Christ, Jesus can change that. The move from "no fruit" to "some fruit" requires repentance. Jesus said to a church that had become apathetic and barren, "Remember then how far you have fallen; repent, and do the works you did at first" (Rev. 2:5a).

Repentance means acknowledging that you've wandered from God and making a u-turn back to Him. First John 1:9 gives us a tremendous promise: "If we confess our sins, he is faithful and righteous to forgive us our sins and to cleanse us from all unrighteousness." If you turn to Jesus and ask Him to forgive and restore you, He will. He will lift you up, clean you off, and restore you to fruitfulness.

Some Fruit: There are also people who are bearing some fruit for Jesus, but they could do much more. "Every branch in me that does not produce fruit he removes, and he prunes every branch that produces fruit so that it will produce more fruit" (John 15:2). This is the person who is sharing his faith and investing in people sometimes—but only when it's convenient. He is serving God occasionally. He could be doing so much more for God's kingdom. Jesus said that this person is unfruitful because he's distracted. Many times people say, "I wish I could really serve God, but I'm so busy." The pace of our lives and the demands of our days often choke out our fruitfulness for God. Jesus put it this way: "All too quickly the message is crowded out by the worries of this life, the lure of wealth, and the desire for other things, so no fruit is produced" (Mark 4:19, NLT). Is this you? Do you find that the busyness of life, the desire for more things, or stress and anxiety rob you of being really fruitful for God?

The move from "some fruit" to "more fruit" requires pruning. Just like a master gardener prunes branches so that a plant can produce more fruit, for our lives to become more fruitful we must be pruned. That may simply mean that you need to prune your schedule. It may require you to thin out your responsibilities to make more time to serve God and invest in others. But in this story, Jesus said the Father is the one doing the pruning. And there are times when God uses trials, hardships, and challenges to prune away the things we hold onto in this life so that we can be fully reliant on Him. Hebrews 12:11 says: "No discipline seems enjoyable at the time, but painful. Later on, however, it yields the peaceful fruit of righteousness to those who have been trained by it." While pruning is painful, if you hold fast to Jesus, you will find that on the other side of the pruning is incredible fruitfulness.

Much Fruit: Finally, Jesus mentions some who are producing more fruit, but they have potential to produce "much fruit" (John 15:5). This is the person who has come through a season of pruning and God is producing fruitfulness. They are seeing people come to Christ; they are investing in people spiritually; and God is at work. But there is still more that God wants to do through this person. He wants to use him or her to produce "much fruit"—fruit that is overflowing and overabundant.

Picture baskets and baskets of fruit. Then picture a huge harvest of people who are touched and transformed by God through this person's life. That is what Jesus has in mind for every one of us. But the move from "more fruit" to "much fruit" requires abiding. Jesus said: "I am the vine; you are the branches. The one who remains in me and I in him produces much fruit, because you can do nothing without me" (John 15:5). Jesus uses the word "remain" eight times in these few verses. The word means "to stay, to dwell, to continue, to make your home with." For a person to be used by God to his or her ultimate potential, it requires abiding with Jesus. It means that you draw close to Him; you spend time in prayer and His Word; you learn what it means to know Him deeply and personally; and you completely rely on His power and strength day by day. Just as branches have to stay vitally connected to the vine so that the life and power to produce fruit can pass through them, we must stay vitally connected with Jesus so that His life and power can work through us to produce fruit that will last for eternity.

Just like a branch that is cut off from the vine eventually withers up and loses its usefulness, when anyone pulls back from Jesus, they fall short of their full redemptive potential. You will never produce much fruit in your own effort. Redemptive fruit only comes by yielding your life to Jesus and asking Him to do in you and through you what only He can do!

What stage of fruitfulness are you in right now?

What do you need to do to move to the next stage of fruitfulness?

What will it cost you to produce "much fruit" for Jesus?

THE FRUITFUL LIFE

You may be thinking, *I want my life to make a difference. I want to bear fruit that will last for eternity, but I'm not sure how to do that.* First John 2:6 says, "Whoever claims to live in him must live as Jesus did" (NIV). Jesus is our model for fruitful living, so living a fruitful life is really living a life that models the life of Jesus. Let's get practical here for a minute. If you want to live a fruitful life by making disciples who make disciples, there are three simple things Jesus did that you need to do.

1. Walk with God. Jesus lived in close fellowship and prayerful dependence on His Father. He spent time in prayer with His Father (see Mark 1:35). Jesus lived in complete reliance on His Father (John 5:19,30). If you want to live the fruitful life, it begins by drawing close to Jesus. Jesus put it this way, "Remain in me" (John 15:4). This means that every day you're seeking to draw close to Jesus by saturating your life with prayer and God's Word, drawing up nourishment from Him and allowing Him to speak to you and lead you. It also means that you place Jesus first in your life (see Matt. 6:33) and live to please Him (see 2 Cor. 5:9,15). Over the three and half years of Jesus' ministry, He was teaching His disciples to love Him and rely on Him for everything. Then when He left He promised He would not leave them alone, but He would send another counselor just like Himself, His Spirit, to be with them forever (see John 14:15-18). As you walk in step with the Spirit, He will guide you and lead you to real fruitfulness (see Gal. 5:16,25).

Set a regular time daily to meet with God. Establish a plan to read God's Word every day and seek His face. Get involved in a local church and make worshiping and serving God a priority.

> *What does it mean to walk with God?*

> *Jesus taught that walking with God is more about loving Him, relying on Him, and abiding in Him for everything rather than asking, "What can I do for God today?" Do you struggle with this thinking? Why or why not?*

2. Reach the lost. Jesus pursued people who were far from God. In fact, Jesus said His purpose for coming was "to seek and to save the lost" (Luke 19:10). Jesus loved people. He knew that people mattered to the Father and they mattered to Him, too. He went out of His way to strike up spiritual conversations with all kinds of people. Later, Jesus said to His disciples, "As the Father has sent me, I also send you" (John 20:21). Jesus spent three and half years training the disciples to actively share the gospel with people who had yet to say yes to Jesus. They became passionate sharers of the gospel, and many people came to Christ as a result of their courage. As you are walking with God, begin to pursue people in your life who don't know Christ. You can begin by writing down the names of four or five people who don't know Jesus. Start praying for them daily. Engage them in conversation. Invite them out to eat and find out what's going on in their lives. Begin to care for their needs and share with them how Jesus has changed your life. You may want to invite them to church with you. As the Spirit leads, share with them how they can come to know Jesus personally. The apostle Paul said, "For I am not ashamed of the gospel, because it is the power of God for salvation to everyone who believes, first to the Jew, and also to the Greek" (Rom. 1:16).

Think of someone in your life who models boldness when it comes to sharing his or her faith. What attributes enable this person to speak so boldly for Christ?

3. Invest in a few. When you look at the life of Jesus, He made it a priority to invest in a few people for maximum impact. The majority of Jesus' ministry was not spent preaching to the crowds, but investing in a few. He taught them to love God. He taught them how to pray and read God's Word. He taught them how to share the gospel and stand strong under trials. He taught them how to make disciples who would make disciples and eventually change the course of history. The vision Jesus had for His disciples is the vision He has for your life. In many ways, your life is like a stone thrown into a still lake. It makes a splash for a moment, but then it quickly disappears. It leaves behind ripples that continue to go on until they reach the shore. When you invest your life in a few people and train them to do the same, you're creating ripples that continue long after you're gone! God wants to use you to create a movement of multiplication that will continue to reach people and invest in people long after you leave this world. That happens as you disciple one life at a time. Ask God to give you one person every six months to disciple. Take this resource and walk someone else through it. Then, challenge them to do the same. Making disciples is how we glorify God and how we fulfill the purpose Jesus has for our lives!

What action steps will you take this week to invest in someone's life? Be specific.

THE DOCTRINE OF GOD

God is the Triune Creator on
mission to redeem the world.

REFLECT

In the previous session, we saw that disciples of Jesus are expected to produce fruit. Specifically, we're called to demonstrate the spiritual fruit of the Holy Spirit's work in our lives as individuals—we are to become more and more like Christ in our character and behavior. We're also called to reproduce more disciples of Jesus through the process of discipleship.

Over the next several sessions, we'll take a closer look at some of the key doctrines of the Christian faith, starting with the doctrine of God. Use the following questions to begin this session with discussion.

Which of the assignments did you explore this week? How did it go?

What did you learn or experience while reading the Bible?

What questions would you like to ask?

PRAY

Begin the session by connecting with God through prayer. Use the following guidelines as you speak with Him:

- Thank God for the opportunity to join with other disciples of Jesus in order to explore the critical doctrines expressed in His Word.

- Praise God for the wisdom and truth expressed in every page of the Bible.

- Ask for wisdom and understanding as you seek to gain a deeper understanding of God's character and role in the world.

INTRODUCTION

A. W. Tozer once wrote, "What comes into our minds when we think about God is the most important thing about us."[1] That is certainly true. God is the Creator and Sustainer of all things; therefore, we cannot be anything or accomplish anything that transcends our connection with Him.

Still, it's important in a study like this one to remember that *thinking* about God is only the beginning. Believing information about God with our heads is only one part of forming a relationship with Him. We must also develop that relationship through our hearts— through our emotions and affections.

In this way, our relationship with God should resemble the sun, which produces both *light* and *heat*. Take a moment to think about our solar system. If the sun produced nothing but light, our planet would be an illuminated wasteland of solid ice. If the sun produced nothing but heat, the lovely diversity of our world would be shrouded in darkness. Only the combination of light and heat produces life.

Those who embrace an intellectual understanding of God may have proper doctrine. However, beliefs won't do us any good if they fail to push us toward an actual love and appreciation of our Creator. Similarly, today's culture is filled with people who demonstrate a genuine passion for spiritual principles and ideas, yet direct that passion toward false idols or false ideas about God. Both approaches are ultimately unfulfilling.

What are the practical consequences of focusing too much on the intellectual side of following God?

What are the practical consequences of focusing too much on our emotions and passion?

As we'll see in this session, God has revealed Himself as the Triune Creator—three separate Persons who make up one Being—who is on a mission to redeem the world. That's a critical doctrine that all disciples of Jesus need to understand. Yet even as you engage the light of the Scriptures throughout this study, don't forget to allow the warmth of God's love to penetrate your own heart. Both are necessary.

KNOW THE STORY

The first words in the Bible are, "In the beginning" (Gen. 1:1). Looking at verse 1 in the Scripture below, it's clear that John wanted to make a bold statement at the beginning of his Gospel. In many ways, John 1 serves as a restatement of Genesis 1.

Not surprisingly, these verses can teach us a great deal about the character of God.

> ¹ In the beginning was the Word,
> and the Word was with God,
> and the Word was God.
> ² He was with God in the beginning.
> ³ All things were created through him,
> and apart from him not one thing was created
> that has been created.
> ⁴ In him was life,
> and that life was the light of men. ...
>
> ¹¹ He came to his own,
> and his own people did not receive him.
> ¹² But to all who did receive him,
> he gave them the right to be children of God,
> to those who believe in his name,
> ¹³ who were born,
> not of natural descent,
> or of the will of the flesh,
> or of the will of man,
> but of God.
> ¹⁴ The Word became flesh
> and dwelt among us.
> We observed his glory,
> the glory as the one and only Son from the Father,
> full of grace and truth.
> JOHN 1:1-4,11-14

What do these verses teach us about God?

UNPACK THE STORY

GOD IS THE TRIUNE CREATOR

In the very first verse of his Gospel, the apostle John made a crucial declaration that's easy to miss if you're not looking for it. Here it is:

> In the beginning was the Word,
> and the Word was with God,
> and the Word was God.
> JOHN 1:1

When John wrote about "the Word," he was actually talking about Jesus. That's why verse 14 says "the Word became flesh and dwelt among us." So, the crucial declaration John made in verse 1 is that Jesus is God. According to this Gospel, Jesus and God are the same Being.

All of this points to a foundational aspect of God's nature: He is the Trinity. The Father, the Son (Jesus), and the Holy Spirit are all one God. Together they form the Deity who created everything out of nothing. Put another way, you can describe God as one "what" and three "who's." He is one Essence, one Being, who exists in three Persons. So, if someone asks you whether God is one or three, the best response is, "Yes."

If we believe God to be infinite and all-powerful, we should never expect to condense Him into a formula we can understand.

What, if anything, have you been taught about the nature of the Trinity?

What questions would you like to ask about the Trinity?

The doctrine of the Trinity is something theologians have historically called an incommunicable aspect of God. Meaning, it's something that human beings cannot grasp. This shouldn't surprise us or even insult us. After all, if we believe God to be infinite and all-powerful, we should never expect to condense Him into a formula we can understand.

How do you respond to the concept of an "incommunicable aspect of God"?

GOD HAS A MISSION TO REDEEM THE WORLD

While it's a challenge to contemplate God's nature as three Persons interconnected within a single Being, we have an easier time identifying God's motives when it comes to us and our world. All we have to do is follow the verbs. For example, when we look at the verbs in Genesis 1, it's clear that God was focused on creating the different elements of our world:

- "Then God said, 'Let there be light,' and there was light" (v. 3).
- "So God created the large sea-creatures and every living creature that moves and swarms in the water, according to their kinds" (v. 21).
- "Then God said, 'Let us make man in our image, according to our likeness'" (v. 26).

What about John 1? If this chapter was constructed as a restatement of Genesis 1, what did the apostle John want to communicate about God's mission and motives?

Read through John 1:11-14 again. What do these verses teach us about God's mission and motives?

One of the main messages of the Bible is that God's creative work in Genesis 1 was eventually corrupted by the presence of human sinfulness. What God created as "good" and "very good" became broken and stained. It makes sense, then, that John's Gospel begins with God's heart to redeem and repair the damage of our sin.

The verbs are fascinating: "He *came* to His own" (v. 11). "He *gave* them the right to be children of God" (v. 12). "The Word *became* flesh" (v. 14). Each of these terms shines a spotlight on God's mission to redeem the world and offer salvation to all people. The verbs reveal an active mission, as well. God didn't remain distant and arrange for our salvation from heaven. He jumped into our world to rescue it and us.

God didn't remain distant and arrange for our salvation from heaven. He jumped into our world to rescue it and us.

How would you describe your first encounters with God?

As you continue through this study, remember that mission and salvation are not simply things God does; they are a part of who He is. God delighted in saving you because He loves you, that's true. But also God is a Savior at His core—so much that He willingly sacrificed Himself for us.

ENGAGE

As disciples of Jesus, evangelism is one of the duties to which we've been called. We have a responsibility to proclaim the message of the gospel within our spheres of influence—to help people understand who God is and what He has done.

Unfortunately, we can't "explain" God in the same way we can explain a math problem or the best way to bake an apple pie. He is God! What we can do, however, is help people understand the basic elements of God's nature and character—and then work to help them experience Him for themselves.

With that in mind, the image below offers a starting point for helping others to begin thinking through the doctrine of the Trinity. Work as a group to practice drawing out the image. Also practice explaining the basic idea of the Trinity to one another so that you'll be ready to help others who want to gain a better understanding of who God is and what He has done.

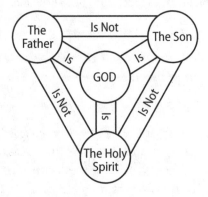

PRAYER REQUESTS

....
....
....
....
....
....
....

1. A. W. Tozer, *The Knowledge of the Holy* (New York: Harper Collins, 1961), 1.

In addition to studying God's Word, work with your group leader to create a plan for personal study, worship, and application between now and the next session. Select from the following optional activities to match your personal preferences and available time.

⬆ Worship

☑ Read your Bible. Complete the reading plan on page 98.

☐ Spend time with God by engaging the devotional experience on page 99.

☐ Connect with God each day through prayer.

➡ ⬅ Personal Study

☐ Read and interact with "God Is the Triune Creator" on page 100.

☐ Read and interact with "God Has a Mission to Redeem the World" on page 102.

⬅ ➡ Application

☐ Take some time to study God's Word and worship Him in a natural setting. Consider what you can learn about God from the world He created.

☐ Memorize Isaiah 40:28: "Do you not know? Have you not heard? The LORD is the everlasting God, the Creator of the whole earth. He never becomes faint or weary; there is no limit to his understanding."

☐ Make an intentional effort to draw and explain the Trinity chart (see p. 96) for someone before the next session.

☐ Start a journal to record your reflections on the different doctrines you'll explore throughout this study. Commit to thinking about what you learn from each session, and then record your questions and insights for later discussion.

☐ Other:

↑ WORSHIP

READING PLAN

Read through the following Scripture passages this week. Use the space provided to record your thoughts and responses.

Day 1
Genesis 1:1-31

Day 2
Exodus 33:12–34:9

Day 3
Jeremiah 10:1-16

Day 4
John 16:12-33

Day 5
Romans 1:18-32

Day 6
Hebrews 8:1-13

Day 7
Revelation 4:1-11

DIVINE TESTIMONY

There's no greater authority on who God is than God Himself. That's why God's Word is the best place to find information about God's nature and character. In the following passage, for example, God takes the incredible step of revealing a piece of Himself to Moses after the exodus from Egypt:

> 5 The LORD came down in a cloud, stood with him there, and proclaimed his name, "the LORD." 6 The LORD passed in front of him and proclaimed: "The LORD—the LORD is a compassionate and gracious God, slow to anger and abounding in faithful love and truth, 7 maintaining faithful love to a thousand generations, forgiving iniquity, rebellion, and sin. But he will not leave the guilty unpunished, bringing the fathers' iniquity on the children and grandchildren to the third and fourth generation."
> EXODUS 34:5-7

Use the following questions to help you reflect on this passage.

What do these verses teach you about God?

How have you recently experienced one of God's characteristics described in these verses?

What aspect of God's character would you like to experience more fully in your life?

Of course, the best way to learn about God is to experience Him through real and personal encounters. Spend several minutes in prayer. Proclaim your desire to know more about Him and to experience Him in a meaningful way. Then be silent. Allow yourself to listen for the voice of His Spirit and feel the reality of His presence with you.

GOD IS THE TRIUNE CREATOR

One of the interesting aspects of studying the Trinity in Scripture is that you'll never find the word *Trinity* in Scripture—not even in the original Hebrew or Greek languages. Indeed, *Trinity* is a term that Bible scholars created in order to discuss God's existence as three distinct Persons united in a single Being.

However, that doesn't mean the concept of the Trinity is foreign or the Scriptures are outside the boundaries of biblical doctrine. In fact, the presence of the Trinity can be felt throughout the entirety of God's Word—starting with the beginning:

> ¹ In the beginning God created the heavens and the earth. ² Now the earth was formless and empty, darkness covered the surface of the watery depths, and the Spirit of God was hovering over the surface of the waters. ³ Then God said, "Let there be light," and there was light.
> GENESIS 1:1-3

The very first verses of the Bible make direct references to God the Father and God the Holy Spirit. But Jesus is there, too, if you know where to look. Remember what John wrote in the first verses of his Gospel:

> ¹ In the beginning was the Word,
> and the Word was with God,
> and the Word was God.
> ² He was with God in the beginning.
> ³ All things were created through him,
> and apart from him not one thing was created
> that has been created·
> JOHN 1:1-3

How do these verses influence your understanding of Genesis 1:1-3?

Because we are created in God's image (see Gen. 1:26-27), what does the nature of the Trinity say about us?

Perhaps the clearest representation of the Trinity occurred during Jesus' baptism at the very beginning of His public ministry:

> [16] When Jesus was baptized, he went up immediately from the water. The heavens suddenly opened for him, and he saw the Spirit of God descending like a dove and coming down on him.
>
> [17] And a voice from heaven said: "This is my beloved Son, with whom I am well-pleased."
> MATTHEW 3:16-17

Again, it's difficult for us to fully process what is happening in these verses. On the one hand, we can see three distinct persons acting in different ways—Jesus was baptized as a human being, the Holy Spirit descended from above in the form of a dove, and God the Father spoke an audible pronouncement of His pleasure with Jesus. At the same time, we know that all three of those Persons exist as one Being. All three are God at the same time.

That's the mystery of the Trinity.

Read the following passages of Scripture and record how they contribute to your understanding of the Trinity.

Matthew 28:18-20

John 14:23-26

2 Corinthians 13:11-13

GOD HAS A MISSION TO REDEEM THE WORLD

When we think about the doctrine of God, we are really attempting to address two major questions: What is God like? What does God do?

How would you answer these questions right now?

The short answer to the first question is: "the Trinity." As we've seen, it's understandably difficult for human beings to process the nature and character of God. The best way we can describe what He is like is three distinct Persons living in perfect community as a single Being. That's the Trinity.

The short answer to the second question is: "just about everything." God created everything in the universe, and He is solely responsible for sustaining everything He created. God is both the source of all things and the ultimate purpose for all things. And that's only a part of what He does. It's also true that, since God exists as a perfect community, another part of what He does is enjoy a relationship with Himself—and with everything He has created.

The Bible helps us understand these big-picture concepts, but that's not its primary focus. Instead, the Scriptures are mainly focused on one specific aspect of what God does. Namely, they help us see God's long-term mission to redeem His creation—including both the world He created and the people He loves.

As you discussed earlier in this session, God's original creation was corrupted by human sin. In response, God initiated a long-term plan designed to re-establish a connection between Himself and humanity—a plan that culminated in Jesus Christ. John offered a helpful summary of that moment:

> The Word became flesh
> and dwelt among us.
> We observed his glory,
> the glory as the one and only Son from the Father,
> full of grace and truth.
> JOHN 1:14

Read the following passages of Scripture and record what they teach about God's mission to redeem the world:

Genesis 12:1-3

Leviticus 26:3-17

Jeremiah 31:31-34

Matthew 28:16-20

Revelation 21:1-8

The total message of the Bible makes it clear that God has personally involved Himself in the mission to restore His creation. He's not a "divine Watchmaker" who created the universe only to remain distant from whatever happens within it. He's not an angry Creator waiting on the edge of His seat to destroy us for our disobedience.

Instead, God has lovingly and patiently worked with us and extended Himself toward us in order to redeem us and restore our relationship with Him.

What are some ways God's mission is evident today?

THE DOCTRINE OF HUMANITY

Human dignity has been distorted by depravity.

REFLECT

In the previous session we looked at the doctrine of God. We saw that God is the Triune Creator—that He exists as one Being in three Persons. We also saw that God has a mission to redeem our broken world. This is consistent with His character because redemption isn't just something God does; it's a major part of who He is. He is a Savior.

As you prepare to explore the doctrine of humanity, take a moment to reflect on your experiences in recent days.

Which of the assignments did you explore this week? How did it go?

What did you learn or experience while reading the Bible?

What questions would you like to ask?

PRAY

Take a break from your discussion and approach God together in prayer. Use the following guidelines as you connect with Him:

- Praise God for the dignity and value you have received as someone created in His image.

- Ask God to speak to you through this session and reveal a new truth to you from His Word.

- Pray that God would soften the hearts of you and your group members to the reality that you need a Savior.

INTRODUCTION

Imagine you're sitting down at a potter's wheel. You scoop the raw, gray clay out of the worn bucket beside you. Slowly, you begin to pour water on the clay as you manipulate the pedals at your feet to start turning the wheel. As the blob of clay begins to spin, you use your hands to shape the clay. Clumpy, hard parts begin to smooth out as you apply just the right amount of pressure. As you cut off the excess material, your lump of clay starts to resemble a small jar.

Your eyes are focused. Your hands are steady. The vision in your mind is becoming reality.

As you're working at the wheel, maybe you envision a day when this jar will be painted and used in your kitchen. Or maybe you dream of giving this handmade pottery to a friend as a gift. There are so many uses for this clump of clay.

But then something goes wrong. The clay collapses, the image is distorted, and the dream of using this clay for its purpose dies. What will you do? Will you scrap the clay altogether and start over with a new batch? Maybe you can remake the clay into something else. Maybe the clay is still valuable and useful.

This was the image the prophet Jeremiah saw when he visited a potter's house. The master craftsman was at the wheel, working deliberately, intentionally, and patiently. But then the clay was marred; the design was ruined in his hands. Yet the potter didn't scrap the clay. Instead he reshaped it into something beautiful. Then Jeremiah heard these words: " 'Can I not treat you as this potter treats his clay?' — this is the LORD's declaration. 'Just like clay in the potter's hand, so are you in my hand, house of Israel' " (Jer. 18:6).

Read Jeremiah 18:1-12. How does the story of the potter's wheel reflect our relationship with God?

What circumstances or modern realities best illustrate how God's creation has been marred by sin?

Let's continue exploring God's interaction with His prize creations—human beings—as we move into the key text for this session.

KNOW THE STORY

To understand the doctrine of humanity, we need to go back to the beginning. The Book of Genesis describes God's creation of the universe and our world—including human beings. It also shows us the exact moment when everything went wrong.

25 So God made the wildlife of the earth according to their kinds, the livestock according to their kinds, and all the creatures that crawl on the ground according to their kinds. And God saw that it was good. 26 Then God said, "Let us make man in our image, according to our likeness. They will rule the fish of the sea, the birds of the sky, the livestock, the whole earth, and the creatures that crawl on the earth." 27 So God created man in his own image; he created him in the image of God; he created them male and female.
GENESIS 1:25-27

1 Now the serpent was the most cunning of all the wild animals that the LORD God had made. He said to the woman, "Did God really say, 'You can't eat from any tree in the garden'?" 2 The woman said to the serpent, "We may eat the fruit from the trees in the garden. 3 But about the fruit of the tree in the middle of the garden, God said, 'You must not eat it or touch it, or you will die.' " 4 "No! You will not die," the serpent said to the woman. 5 "In fact, God knows that when you eat it your eyes will be opened and you will be like God, knowing good and evil." 6 The woman saw that the tree was good for food and delightful to look at, and that it was desirable for obtaining wisdom. So she took some of its fruit and ate it; she also gave some to her husband, who was with her, and he ate it.
GENESIS 3:1-6

What do you like best about our world? Why?

In what ways has sin most dramatically affected your family?

UNPACK THE STORY

EXPLORING HUMAN DIGNITY

When we think about the creation of human beings, and even what it means to be human, Genesis 1:25-26 offers a key distinction:

> ²⁵ So God made the wildlife of the earth according to their kinds, the livestock according to their kinds, and all the creatures that crawl on the ground according to their kinds. And God saw that it was good. ²⁶ Then God said, "Let us make man in our image, according to our likeness. They will rule the fish of the sea, the birds of the sky, the livestock, the whole earth, and the creatures that crawl on the earth."
> GENESIS 1:25-26

When God created the animals, He created them "according to their kinds." And as He created, He developed new and distinct patterns so that each type of animal was designed according to its own kind.

Things were different when God created human beings. In that case, He didn't create a new mold or pattern. Instead, He made humans according to *His own* kind. God created us as a reflection of Himself—of His own image. In other words, God was the pattern. This is what makes people distinctly different from the rest of creation but at the same time clearly a part of it. We are higher than the animals, yet still not God. This truth guides our understanding through the rest of God's Word because it helps us know who we are and what our purpose is.

Even better, these verses teach us about our value. Because we are created in God's image, we have dignity. We have worth. Unrelated to anything we do or will do—without any asterisks or caveats—we have value because we are reflections of God.

> Because we are created in God's image, we have dignity. We have worth. Unrelated to anything we do or will do—without any asterisks or caveats—we have value because we are reflections of God.

What are the implications of people being made in the image of God?

How should this truth influence our actions and attitudes?

EXPLORING HUMAN DEPRAVITY

While mankind was created in dignity, it didn't last. Human dignity was quickly marred by depravity, which is the presence of sin. Just as Jeremiah's clay was marred in the potter's hands, our lives have been corrupted by disobedience and sin.

What comes to mind when you hear the word "sin"? Why?

The ancient Hebrew word translated as *sin* is actually an archery term. It means "to miss the mark" or "to fall short of the goal." When we disobey God, we miss the mark of His intended purpose for our lives. We fall short of God's plan.

And there are consequences.

Read Romans 3:23; Ephesians 2:1-3; and Colossians 2:13a. Then describe the consequences of sin in our lives.

Sin is like a virus that has infected every person. It's a global epidemic. While God created human beings as "good" and with the wonderful capacity to know Him, enjoy Him, serve Him, and love Him, sin distorted who we are. People are now depraved. We are corrupt morally and wayward from God.

The result of our sin is separation from God in this life and divine judgment for our sin in the next. There is nothing we can do to change ourselves or save ourselves. Only Someone from outside of this sinful world can save us.

> There is nothing we can do to change ourselves or save ourselves. Only Someone from outside of this sinful world can save us.

Continue reading Romans 3:23-24; Ephesians 2:4-5; and Colossians 2:13b. Then discuss the solution each passage offers for the problem of sin.

ENGAGE

As you continue to study the major doctrines of the Christian faith, you'll benefit from finding ways to identify and apply those doctrines in everyday life. With that in mind, work with your group to assess the Bible's claims about humanity in light of current events.

Use the following questions to gauge how well the doctrine of humanity compares with what is happening in the world today. Consider looking through news sources (in print or online) in order to identify current events that reflect the human condition, both positive and negative. Examples could include anything from trials, crimes, and diseases all the way to prizes, works of art, and displays of heroism. (*Note:* if you don't have any news sources available, consider engaging this activity on your own in the next few days.)

Where do you see the dignity of humanity reflected in current events?

Where do you see the depravity of humanity reflected in current events?

PRAYER REQUESTS

In addition to studying God's Word, work with your group leader to create a plan for personal study, worship, and application between now and the next session. Select from the following optional activities to match your personal preferences and available time.

⬆ Worship

☑ Read your Bible. Complete the reading plan on page 112.

☐ Spend time with God by engaging the devotional experience on page 113.

☐ Take a walk this week and enjoy God's creation. Then sit down and craft your own psalm of worship to God.

➡ ⬅ Personal Study

☐ Read and interact with "Everyone Is Valuable" on page 114.

☐ Read and interact with "Everything Is Worship" on page 116.

⬅ ➡ Application

☐ Take time this week to share with someone your personal faith story. Start by telling them what your life was like before you met Jesus. Then tell them how you came to faith in Christ. Follow that with the difference Jesus has made in your life today.

☐ Take a moment to journal about the following: King David was confronted by his own personal sin. In a dramatic moment, the cover up of his elicit affair and the murder of Bathsheba's husband were exposed. There was nowhere to hide. In that moment, David was a broken man. He poured out his heart to God in his own personal journal. Read Psalm 51. How did David see his sin? What did he say to God? Take a moment to write your own journal entry of confession to God.

☐ Memorize Romans 3:23: "For all have sinned and fall short of the glory of God."

☐ Other:

WORSHIP

READING PLAN

Read through the following Scripture passages this week. Use the space provided to record your thoughts and responses.

Day 1
Genesis 1:24-31

Day 2
Psalm 8:1-9

Day 3
Romans 7:13-25

Day 4
Isaiah 43:1-7

Day 5
Psalm 139:1-24

Day 6
Ephesians 4:17-24

Day 7
Psalm 119:73-80

PRONE TO WANDER

We all went astray like sheep; we all have turned to our own way.
ISAIAH 53:6

Sheep have a tendency to wander. No matter how you speak to them, no matter how you train them, they are innately prone to wander away from their shepherd. In many ways, people act the same way. We also are prone to wander.

Robert Robinson grew up in a broken family. His father died when he was young, and he was sent out to work hard labor jobs early in life. He fell into the wrong crowd and soon ran the streets with wild company. It is said, that night as he and his friends were harassing an old gypsy woman, she pointed at Robert and said, "You will live to see your children and grandchildren." That got his attention. He thought, *If I'm going to live to see my children and grandchildren, I need to change the way I'm living.*

On another occasion, Robinson joined his friends to hear George Whitefield speak. They went with the intention of heckling the crowd, but that night Robert heard the gospel of Jesus Christ for the first time. He surrendered his life to the Savior. Two years later, in 1757, Robinson wrote down the lyrics to a hymn that is still sung in churches today: "Come, Thou Fount of Every Blessing."

In the last stanza, Robert wrote these words:

> Prone to wander, Lord, I feel it,
> Prone to leave the God I love;
> Here's my heart, Lord, take and seal it;
> Seal it for Thy courts above.[1]

Like Robert, and like sheep, there is something inside all human beings that causes us to drift from God. Our sin veers us off course and lures us from the One we love.

Describe a time in your life when you have wandered from God.

How has God brought you back to Himself?

EVERYONE IS VALUABLE

Many people think the sole purpose of Genesis 1–2 is to tell us how old the earth is. Simply put, Genesis isn't given to us for that. It isn't given to us to understand *how* or *when* the world was created. It's given to us to tell us *Who* created the universe and *why* He created it. Take a closer look at Genesis 1:26-28:

> 26 Then God said, "Let us make man in our image, according to our likeness. They will rule the fish of the sea, the birds of the sky, the livestock, the whole earth, and the creatures that crawl on the earth." 27 So God created man in his own image; he created him in the image of God; he created them male and female. 28 God blessed them, and God said to them, "Be fruitful, multiply, fill the earth, and subdue it. Rule the fish of the sea, the birds of the sky, and every creature that crawls on the earth."
> GENESIS 1:26-28

What would you identify as the primary theme of these verses?

Notice that this was the first time in the creation account that God said "Let us." The Father, Son, and Holy Spirit are involved in the creation of mankind. There isn't just a physical creation happening here. There's spiritual creation happening as well. You are physical like the animals, but don't forget you are also spiritual—patterned after God to do and be something higher than the animals. But what does it mean to be patterned after God or created in the "image of God"? Consider the following statements.

People are created in God's image mentally. Just as God is rational, volitional, and communicative, mankind was created to reason, choose, and communicate. Every time a person thinks through a problem, chooses a course of action, or crafts a painting, he or she is reflecting the image of God.

People are created in God's image morally. Just as God is holy (see Isa. 6:3), righteous (see Ps. 145:17), just (see 2 Thess. 1:6), and good (see Ps. 136:1), God created mankind with a "moral compass" to choose right from wrong—a conscience (see Rom. 2:15) to make moral choices.

People are created in God's image socially. Just as God exists in community as the Trinity (Father, Son, and Spirit), God created people to live in community. The declaration that it was "not good for the man to be alone" (Gen. 2:18) represents our need for relationships with other people and with God. We can know God in a personal way and can choose to talk to Him in prayer, worship Him, serve Him, and obey Him.

People are created in God's image eternally. Just as God is eternal, mankind was created to live eternally. Although people have a finite beginning, each person is created with a living soul (Gen. 2:7), an immaterial part of his or her being that will live forever either with God or apart from God.

Which of the previous statements do you find the most difficult to believe? Why?

The dignity of mankind is that God has personally, uniquely, and purposefully created each person for His own pleasure and for His own glory (see Isa. 43:7). Every person matters to God (see Matt. 10:31). Every person possesses the image of God (see Gen. 1:26). Every person is a divinely-crafted masterpiece (see Eph. 2:10). Every person is loved by God (see John 3:16). Every person finds satisfaction and joy in knowing God and fulfilling the purpose for which God has given his or her life.

So there is good news and bad news. You've already heard the good news: every single person is valuable—without a caveat and regardless of what we believe about God or what we've done—because we all are created in God's image.

That's good news. The bad news is that every person you hate, disagree with, can't stand to be around, that's ever hurt you, lied to you, manipulated you, or disagreed with you—they are valuable as well. We don't get to believe that some people are image bearers of God and are valuable, while others are not.

And anytime we disagree with that in our actions or words, we are marring the image of God.

Do you have trouble believing the previous statement? Why or why not?

If every person was created by God and matters to God, then every person deserves to be treated with dignity and respect.

What are some ways you can demonstrate dignity and respect to those who have fallen through the cracks in your community?

EVERYTHING IS WORSHIP

We have already established that because humans are all image bearers of God, everyone has value and is significant. If this is true and we are all significant, then everything we do is significant. Everything we do carries meaning. Everything is potentially an act of worship.

This is another good news/bad news situation. The good news is that nothing you do is unimportant. And isn't that attractive? Don't we all want who we are and what we do to count? If this is true, everything you do is designed to picture something true about God.

> The LORD God took the man and placed him in the garden of Eden
> to work it and watch over it.
> GENESIS 2:15

God put the man in this perfect garden and his purpose was to work and keep it. This is a loaded verse. The words *placed, work,* and *watch* have much deeper meanings than simply "God set them down in the garden and then had them tilling the soil and growing plants." The word *placed* means to set at rest. It's a peaceful term. It's like when you (against all your better judgment about how you'll be late, or how messy you'll get, or how risky it is) turn around on the interstate to go back and help that person change their flat tire in the pouring rain. You drive away soaked and late to your appointment with no perceivable benefit to you at all, and you still think, *That was what I was supposed to do.* When God placed the man in the garden, He was setting him at rest—at peace. And what He gave him to do didn't disrupt that rest—it's the very expression of it. See, God told the man to "work it and watch over it"—essentially to worship and obey. This is the expression of deepest rest. The way you are most human, both physical and spiritual, is to worship and obey in whatever state or environment you might find yourself in. This is what it means to reflect God's image. This is what it means to experience His "this is who I'm supposed to be" kind of rest. This is done by worshiping and obeying our Creator.

What observations stand out to you the most about this explanation of Genesis 2:15?

That's the good news. Everything is important because everything is worship. The bad news is this: we're all blowing it. The word *worship* comes from the Old English word *worth-ship*. In other words, what you worship is whatever has ultimate worth in your life. Worshiping God simply means that you put ultimate weight on what He says about you, about life, and about the world. You then put your trust in Him and obey Him.

And though we all worship, most of us end up worshiping ourselves. Worshiping yourself just means the ultimate weight goes onto you—about who you say you are and who you say other people are. But if all of our lives are supposed to reflect God's image, and our ultimate rest comes from believing that God is the only one worthy of obeying, then not a single thing we do should be separated from showing that worth. First Corinthians 10:31 says, "So, whether you eat or drink, or whatever you do, do everything for the glory of God." Remember, everything you do is spiritual. It's heavy. It's important.

What questions come to mind when reading that everything you do has weight and significance?

Paul Tripp describes our worship in this way:

"Human beings were created by God to be worshipers. You can't divide people into two groups, as if there are some who worship and others who don't. Every person, regardless of religious profession, has worshiped their way through every day of their existence. I would even argue that everything you say and everything you do is an act of worship. ... Romans 1:25 is probably the best diagnosis on our worship condition. It says that human beings will exchange the worship of the Creator for worship of created things. ... How are you doing in awareness? Are you sensitive to each opportunity you have to worship in word and deed? And how are you doing in action? Are you frequently exchanging the worship of God for worship of created things? ... For the child of God, life in a fallen world will be one big worship war. Even though we've been given the Holy Spirit and the ability to worship the Creator at all times, our sinful nature will fight to worship the created world."[2]

From Paul Tripp's quote, what application can you make to your life today?

1. Robert Robinson, "Come, Thou Fount of Every Blessing," *The Worship Hymnal* (Nashville, TN: LifeWay Worship, 2008), 98.
2. Paul Tripp, "Worship Everyday," *paultripp.com* [online], 14 July 2014 [accessed 24 April 2015].

THE PERSON AND WORK OF CHRIST

Jesus is God who reconciles us back to God.

REFLECT

We saw in the previous session that human beings were created in God's image and designed to live in relationship with Him. Sadly, God's original plan was corrupted by the presence of sin. Our connection with God has been severed, and there's nothing we can do to fix it on our own. Thankfully, that reality points us to Jesus.

As you prepare to explore both the Person and work of Christ, take a moment to reflect on your experiences in recent days.

Which of the assignments did you explore this week? How did it go?

What did you learn or experience while reading the Bible?

What questions would you like to ask?

PRAY

Take a break from your discussion and approach God together in prayer. Use the following guidelines as you connect with Him:

- As a group, acknowledge the presence of sin in your lives. Take a moment to silently confess your sin before engaging the Scriptures.

- Ask for a greater awareness of the Spirit's presence as you explore God's Word together.

- Praise Jesus for the good news of the gospel and the ways He has changed your life.

INTRODUCTION

Many different people have been influential on a grand scale throughout human history. As we look back across the centuries, we are indebted to men and women who literally changed the course not only of civilizations, but of the entire world.

For example, think back to Alexander the Great. Tutored by Aristotle, a famous philosopher, Alexander has a convincing claim as the most successful military tactician in the history of the world. By the time he died in his early 30's, Alexander was undefeated in battle and had conquered a huge territory stretching from Egypt and Greece all the way to the borders of India. Even after his death, Alexander's work was vital in spreading Greek culture throughout much of the world, and his conquests laid the foundation for the later rise of the Roman Empire.

Johannes Gutenberg was another hugely influential figure in history, although his contributions were much different than those of Alexander the Great. Gutenberg invented the movable type printing press in the middle of the 15th century, which ushered in a new era of mass communication, increased literacy, and the facilitated the spread of radical ideas, such as Protestant theology and nation-based languages.

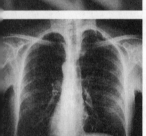

Moving closer to our time, Marie Curie serves as one of the world's most influential scientists. Marie was awarded the Nobel Prize on two separate occasions and in two separate fields—chemistry and physics. Her discoveries in radioactivity paved the way for modern practices such as x-ray machines and radiation therapy.

Who are some of your favorite people from history? Why?

Of course, thinking about important people in the past reminds us of an important truth: Jesus Christ is without a doubt the most influential person in the history of the world. As we'll see in the following pages, Jesus' impact in the world can be traced to both who He is and what He has done.

Where do you see evidence of Jesus' influence throughout the world today?

KNOW THE STORY

Everyone seems to have an opinion of who Jesus is and what He sought to accomplish during His time on earth. Fortunately, we don't have to rely on the opinions of others. Jesus Himself has revealed the truth throughout the Bible—including this declaration at the beginning of His public ministry:

[16] He came to Nazareth, where he had been brought up. As usual, he entered the synagogue on the Sabbath day and stood up to read. [17] The scroll of the prophet Isaiah was given to him, and unrolling the scroll, he found the place where it was written:

> [18] The Spirit of the Lord is on me,
> because he has anointed me
> to preach good news to the poor.
> He has sent me
> to proclaim release to the captives
> and recovery of sight to the blind,
> to set free the oppressed,
> [19] to proclaim the year of the Lord's favor.

[20] He then rolled up the scroll, gave it back to the attendant, and sat down. And the eyes of everyone in the synagogue were fixed on him. [21] He began by saying to them, "Today as you listen, this Scripture has been fulfilled."
LUKE 4:16-21

[28] When they heard this, everyone in the synagogue was enraged. [29] They got up, drove him out of town, and brought him to the edge of the hill that their town was built on, intending to hurl him over the cliff. [30] But he passed right through the crowd and went on his way.
LUKE 4:28-30

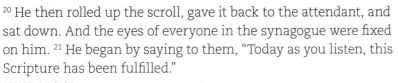

What do these verses communicate about who Jesus is and what He does?

UNPACK THE STORY

JESUS IS FULLY GOD AND FULLY HUMAN

As we explore the Person of Jesus and attempt to identify who He is, one of the first truths we need to understand is that Jesus is both fully God and fully human. This can be a difficult concept to process. Fortunately, the Scriptures provide some concrete examples that highlight both elements of Jesus' nature.

In Luke 4, for example, we see evidence of Jesus' humanity. Verse 16 says Jesus came to the village of Nazareth, "where he had been brought up." Jesus had a hometown. He had neighbors. He was part of a community. What's more, Jesus had regular patterns and predictable routines:

> As *usual*, he entered the synagogue on the Sabbath day and stood up to read.
> LUKE 4:16b, emphasis added

> Jesus had a hometown. He had neighbors. He was part of a community. What's more, Jesus had regular patterns and predictable routines.

Why is it important to understand that Jesus was fully human?

Luke 4 also provides two interesting pictures of Jesus' divinity—the first of which was initiated by Jesus Himself. After being handed a scroll containing the Book of Isaiah, Jesus chose to read a prophecy about the Messiah. Each of His hearers would have been familiar with this passage, and each would have longed for the prophecy to be fulfilled. So, even reading the passage was suggestive on Jesus' behalf. Yet Jesus left no doubt about His intentions when He declared: "Today as you listen, this Scripture has been fulfilled" (v. 21).

The second illustration of Jesus' divinity came when He miraculously passed through an angry mob. The text makes it clear that the people of Jesus' hometown were enraged to the point of murder (see v. 29). Yet Jesus passed through them as if they weren't even there. Interestingly, the people weren't angry that Jesus declared Himself the Messiah. Instead, they were enraged at the notion of God accepting the Gentiles and rejecting His chosen people (see vv. 24-30).

Why is it important to understand that Jesus was fully God?

JESUS ACCOMPLISHES OUR SALVATION

Now that we have a greater understanding of Jesus' identity—of who He is—let's take a moment to consider what He does on our behalf. Once again, we have the benefit of Jesus' own words to get us started:

> 18 The Spirit of the Lord is on me,
> because he has anointed me
> to preach good news to the poor.
> He has sent me
> to proclaim release to the captives
> and recovery of sight to the blind,
> to set free the oppressed,
> 19 to proclaim the year of the Lord's favor.
> LUKE 4:18-19

How have you seen these verses fulfilled through Jesus' life and ministry?

On the surface, Jesus' words seem to focus primarily on social issues—good news for the poor, freedom for the captives, sight for the blind, and relief for the oppressed. And it's certainly true that Jesus' ministry in the world has accomplished these goals throughout Christian history.

However, it's vital to understand that Jesus had a deeper meaning in mind. The people of Jesus' day believed the Messiah would restore the glory of Israel in a blaze of military and political power. Yet Jesus knew that His mission was primarily spiritual. He came to proclaim the good news of redemption, to free all people from their captivity to sin, to heal our spiritual blindness, and to set us free from the oppression of our own flesh.

In other words, Jesus came to accomplish our salvation.

How have you personally benefited from Jesus' ministry?

Jesus came to proclaim the good news of redemption, to free all people from their captivity to sin, to heal our spiritual blindness, and to set us free from the oppression of our own flesh.

ENGAGE

One of the important elements involved with studying Christian doctrine is learning to identify teachings and statements that are incorrect. This is especially important in connection with the doctrine of Christ. Throughout history, there have been many false teachers who have spread heresy regarding the Person and work of Jesus. Many of these false doctrines still exist today.

With that in mind, work as a group to answer the following questions.

What are some false teachings about Jesus that remain popular in today's culture? Make a list, if possible.

What steps can we take to properly evaluate different teachings in order to determine whether they are true or false?

PRAYER REQUESTS

WEEKLY ACTIVITIES

In addition to studying God's Word, work with your group leader to create a plan for personal study, worship, and application between now and the next session. Select from the following optional activities to match your personal preferences and available time.

⬆ Worship

☑ Read your Bible. Complete the reading plan on page 126.

☐ Spend time with God by engaging the devotional experience on page 127.

☐ Connect with God each day through prayer.

➡⬅ Personal Study

☐ Read and interact with "Fully Human and Fully God" on page 128.

☐ Read and interact with "Our Salvation" on page 130.

⬅➡ Application

☐ Pray at the beginning of each day that God would open the door for you to share the truth about Jesus with someone who needs to hear it. Keep your eyes open throughout the day for possible answers to your prayers.

☐ Memorize Hebrews 4:15: "For we do not have a high priest who is unable to sympathize with our weaknesses, but one who has been tempted in every way as we are, yet without sin."

☐ When you have an opportunity to participate in Jesus' mission this week, invite another disciple to join you.

☐ Deepen your knowledge of Christian doctrine by seeking more information on the Person and work of Jesus. Read a book, download a podcast, listen to a sermon, etc.

☐ Other:

 **WORSHIP**

READING PLAN

Read through the following Scripture passages this week. Use the space provided to record your thoughts and responses

Day 1
Isaiah 11:1-9

Day 2
Luke 1:26-56

Day 3
John 1:1-18

Day 4
John 19:1-42

Day 5
Philippians 2:1-11

Day 6
Hebrews 2:1-18

Day 7
Revelation 1:1-20

POSITION AND PRACTICE

We often think of Christian doctrines as abstract concepts—complicated theories that don't really apply to everyday life. This isn't true, of course. The doctrines of the Christian faith are essential to everyday life because they help us understand who we are, who we were meant to be, and how we are called to live in service to God. In many ways, Christian doctrine is the foundation of everyday life for a disciple of Christ.

The good news is that doctrine doesn't have to be complicated. Because the doctrines have practical application in our lives, they can be understood in practical terms. For example, consider the following chart as a way of explaining the salvation Christ has accomplished for us:

	Position *What God Sees*	Practice *What We Are*
Non-Christian	Sinful	Sinful
Christian	Righteous	Sinful
Glorified Christian	Righteous	Righteous

As you can see from the chart, all people are defined by their sinful condition before they receive the gift of salvation offered by Jesus. Before we know Christ, we are sinful in what we do and sinful in God's eyes.

When we encounter Jesus, however, something vital changes in our position with God. We continue to practice sin as we go about our lives—Christians don't become perfect when they follow Christ. But because Jesus has taken the penalty for our sins, we are forgiven in our position before God. In fact, when God looks at us, He doesn't see our failing bodies and corrupted minds. Instead, He sees the righteousness of Christ. That's the miracle known as the doctrine of salvation.

Finally, when we shed our sinful flesh through death, we take up new life with Christ in heaven—a process known as "glorification." In this new life, we not only have the position of righteousness in God's eyes, but we also practice righteousness in every moment of our lives. We become like Jesus.

How should the doctrine of salvation influence your actions and attitudes each day?

→ ← PERSONAL STUDY 1

FULLY HUMAN AND FULLY GOD

We use a number of different titles in today's culture for different things. Most of these titles are connected with our jobs—with the things we do. Think of "doctor," "professor," and "judge," for example. People used titles in the ancient world, as well. However, those titles were often connected to who a person was, rather than what a person did. A person's title was a key element of his or her identity.

With that in mind, we can further explore the nature of Jesus' character and identity by focusing on two titles commonly used to identify Him throughout the Scriptures: "Son of God" and "Son of Man."

First, let's look at "Son of God." Interestingly, Jesus rarely used this title when referencing Himself. Instead, others often applied this title to Jesus in order to identify His divine heritage.

> *Read the following passages of Scripture and identify those who proclaimed Jesus to be the "Son of God":*
>
> *Luke 1:35*
>
> *Luke 4:40-41*
>
> *Luke 22:66-71*
>
> *John 1:43-51*

In the culture of Jesus' day, society was heavily influenced by the concepts of sonship and inheritance. Specifically, the eldest son in a family was the primary heir of his father, which meant he carried his father's status and authority. To call Jesus the "Son of God," then, was to give Jesus the same level of honor and authority as God.

Essentially, the title "Son of God" was a declaration that Jesus was equal with God. Given the context of the rest of the Bible, we can say with certainty that Jesus *is* God.

> *Take a moment to skim through the Gospel of Matthew. What evidence do you see to support the claim that Jesus is God?*

Now let's take a deeper look at Jesus' second title: "Son of Man." This was actually the title Jesus used most often when referring to Himself. For example:

> ²⁶ "It must not be like that among you. On the contrary, whoever wants to become great among you must be your servant, ²⁷ and whoever wants to be first among you must be your slave; ²⁸ just as the Son of Man did not come to be served, but to serve, and to give his life as a ransom for many."
> MATTHEW 20:26-28

"Son of Man" emphasizes Jesus' humanity. The title reminds us that since Jesus has a physical body like ours, He also shares our weakness, our frailty, and even our suffering. No pain we experience is unfamiliar to our Lord, and no problem we encounter is too big for His power.

> ¹⁴ Therefore, since we have a great high priest who has passed through the heavens—Jesus the Son of God—let us hold fast to our confession. ¹⁵ For we do not have a high priest who is unable to sympathize with our weaknesses, but one who has been tempted in every way as we are, yet without sin.
> HEBREWS 4:14-15

How does Jesus' humanity impact your life today?

Imagine that a Christian friend of yours has recently been diagnosed with cancer. This friend is facing the real possibility of death and therefore is in great despair.

How would you comfort your friend with the truth that Jesus is fully human?

How would you comfort your friend with the truth that Jesus is fully God?

OUR SALVATION

We've seen that Jesus is both fully human and fully God. He is the "Son of God" and the "Son of Man." This can be a difficult concept to understand in full, but it's a concept that has a vital impact on our spiritual lives. Consider the following:

32 "As for me, if I am lifted up from the earth I will draw all people to myself." 33 He said this to indicate what kind of death he was about to die. 34 Then the crowd replied to him, "We have heard from the law that the Messiah will remain forever. So how can you say, 'The Son of Man must be lifted up'? Who is this Son of Man?" 35 Jesus answered, "The light will be with you only a little longer. Walk while you have the light so that darkness doesn't overtake you. The one who walks in darkness doesn't know where he's going. 36 While you have the light, believe in the light so that you may become children of light."
JOHN 12:32-36a, emphasis added

16 For God loved the world in this way: He gave his one and only Son, so that everyone who believes in him will not perish but have eternal life. 17 For God did not send his Son into the world to condemn the world, but to save the world through him. 18 Anyone who believes in him is not condemned, but anyone who does not believe is already condemned, because he has not believed in the name of *the one and only Son of God*.
JOHN 3:16-18, emphasis added

Jesus' dual nature is a necessary foundation for our salvation. Without His full humanity and full divinity, we would be lost.

Why is Jesus' humanity a necessary element of our salvation?

Why is Jesus' divinity a necessary element of our salvation?

These point back to an Old-Testament event called the Day of Atonement. On this day each year, the high priest chose a lamb upon which to place all the sins of all the people of Israel. This lamb was then sent out to die in the wilderness, bearing away the sins of the people and leaving them clean before God.

This was a ritual, of course. There wasn't anything special about the lamb chosen each year, nor did the priest have any real power to offer forgiveness. Instead, the ritual pointed forward to the coming Someone who *was* special and who *did* have power: Jesus Christ.

With that in mind, look at what John the Baptist said when he first encountered Jesus:

> ²⁹ The next day John saw Jesus coming toward him and said, "Here is the Lamb of God, who takes away the sin of the world! ³⁰ This is the one I told you about: 'After me comes a man who ranks ahead of me, because he existed before me.'"
> JOHN 1:29-30

How do these verses contribute to your understanding of salvation?

The doctrine of atonement is easy to remember when you break it into parts: "at-one-ment." In that single moment ("ment") when Jesus died on the cross, He made us "at one" with God by bearing the punishment for our sins.

Again, it's important to see that only Jesus could accomplish such a feat. Because Jesus is fully human, He was able to take our sins upon Himself—and to die because of it. Yet, since Jesus is fully God, He is larger even than our sins. His power as God allowed Him to absorb our punishment and still rise victorious from the grave.

What steps can you take to worship and thank Jesus for His accomplishments as part of your daily life?

THE KINGDOM OF GOD

God's kingdom includes the "now and not yet" reign of King Jesus.

REFLECT

We saw in the previous session that Jesus Christ is both fully human and fully God. This dual nature is at the core of Christ's identity, and it points to His primary reason for coming to earth: securing our salvation. Jesus alone accomplishes salvation for those within God's kingdom.

But what *is* God's kingdom? That's the focus of this session. Before we dive in, however, take a moment to discuss your recent experiences.

Which of the assignments did you explore this week? How did it go?

What did you learn or experience while reading the Bible?

What questions would you like to ask?

PRAY

Take a break from your discussion and approach God together in prayer. Use the following guidelines as you connect with Him:

- As a group, take a moment to praise and honor Jesus as the King of the universe.

- Confess that you often live as if you were outside of God's kingdom—as if you were king of your life, rather than God. Ask Him to forgive your sins.

- Ask for wisdom as you study what it means to live as a member of God's kingdom and help advance His kingdom in the world.

INTRODUCTION

How many kingdoms are you in charge of? Unless you're currently leading one of the 40 or so monarchies in existence throughout the world, your first answer to that question is probably, "None." But don't be so sure!

In its truest form, a "kingdom" is simply any place in which a person's will is done. If a man is in charge of a country—if his will is carried out within its borders—that country is his kingdom. In the same way, if a businesswoman is in charge of a company, that company is essentially her kingdom. An estate owner who tells resources where to go and what to do has a kingdom. Even a child who is allowed to make decisions about his or her bedroom has a tiny kingdom.

In short, wherever your will is carried out, that is your kingdom.

What are some "kingdoms" you're in charge of?

What have you learned or been taught about the kingdom of God?

As we think about the kingdom of God, the same definition for *kingdom* applies. Therefore, God's kingdom exists wherever His will is carried out. To say it in another way, the kingdom of God is simply the reign and rule of God over any area in which He has control.

That's why Jesus included these famous words in His model prayer:

> Your kingdom come.
> Your will be done
> on earth as it is in heaven.
> MATTHEW 6:10-11

As we explore the doctrine of God's kingdom throughout this session, we'll gain a greater understanding of what it means for God's kingdom to come both in this world and in the lives of those who follow Him.

KNOW THE STORY

Many people today feel confused about the kingdom of God. Does God's kingdom exist now, or is it something we will experience in the future? The people of Jesus' day had the same questions:

20 Being asked by the Pharisees when the kingdom of God would come, he answered them, "The kingdom of God is not coming with something observable; 21 no one will say, 'See here!' or 'There!' For you see, the kingdom of God is in your midst."

22 Then he told the disciples: "The days are coming when you will long to see one of the days of the Son of Man, but you won't see it. 23 They will say to you, 'See there!' or 'See here!' Don't follow or run after them. 24 For as the lightning flashes from horizon to horizon and lights up the sky, so the Son of Man will be in his day. 25 But first it is necessary that he suffer many things and be rejected by this generation.

26 "Just as it was in the days of Noah, so it will be in the days of the Son of Man: 27 People went on eating, drinking, marrying and giving in marriage until the day Noah boarded the ark, and the flood came and destroyed them all. 28 It will be the same as it was in the days of Lot: People went on eating, drinking, buying, selling, planting, building. 29 But on the day Lot left Sodom, fire and sulfur rained from heaven and destroyed them all. 30 It will be like that on the day the Son of Man is revealed. …

33 Whoever tries to make his life secure will lose it, and whoever loses his life will preserve it. 34 I tell you, on that night two will be in one bed; one will be taken and the other will be left. 35 Two women will be grinding grain together; one will be taken and the other left."
LUKE 17:20-30,33-35

What do these verses reveal about the kingdom of God?

UNPACK THE STORY

GOD'S KINGDOM IS "NOW AND NOT YET"

Jesus' interaction with the Pharisees in Luke 17 seems uncomplicated. For once, they asked Him a straightforward question: when will the kingdom of God come? And it seems as if Jesus gave them a straightforward answer: "the kingdom of God is in your midst" (v. 21). Yet, when Jesus turned to His disciples in verse 22, He proceeded to describe in some detail what it would be like when the kingdom of God comes in full.

So, what gives? The answer is that God's kingdom is both "now" and "not yet."

One of the core messages of the Bible is that sin has corrupted the relationship between God and humanity. Sin always goes against God's will, which means our sinfulness is a rejection of God's will. And because we have rejected God's will, we are in active rebellion against His kingdom. Remember, God's kingdom exists wherever His will is carried out.

However, sin has not removed everyone from God's kingdom. Beginning with the Israelites and extending to the church, God is carrying out His plan to restore His relationship with humanity by offering us atonement and salvation. When we repent of our sin and submit to Christ as our Lord and Savior, we're no longer in active rebellion against God. We are welcomed back into His kingdom with open arms.

> When we repent of our sin and submit to Christ as our Lord and Savior, we're no longer in active rebellion against God. We are welcomed back into His kingdom with open arms.

What are the benefits and challenges of being members in God's kingdom?

The reason Jesus could say "the kingdom of God is in your midst" is because many people of His time had submitted to God's will. The same is true today, although on a larger scale— what we know as the church. Still, the majority of humanity remains in rebellion against God.

There will come a day, however, when all rebellion will end. God will once again establish His kingdom across the world. This is the time of judgment Jesus described to His disciples.

Look again at Luke 17:26-35. What emotions do you experience when you read these verses?

CHRISTIANS LIVE AS CITIZENS OF GOD'S KINGDOM

In teaching His disciples about the future revelation of God's kingdom, Jesus referenced two stories from the Old Testament that both paint a frightening picture.

> *Read Genesis 7:11-24; 19:12-26. What are your initial reactions to these passages?*

By referencing the stories of Noah and Lot, Jesus was highlighting the sharp contrast between the kingdom of God and the kingdom of the world. In both stories, the majority of people were concerned only with worldly needs and desires: eating, drinking, marrying, buying, selling, planting, building, and so on. These aren't negative activities—they're not sinful in and of themselves—but they are entirely focused on temporary concerns.

Jesus' point is that people who focus only on earthly activities, ignoring God's will in the process, will be blindsided when the day of judgment arrives. In other words, those who belong to the kingdom of the world are ignorant of their spiritual danger because they care only about the kingdom of the world.

Luke 17:33 is the key: "Whoever tries to make his life secure will lose it, and whoever loses his life will preserve it." The only way to move from the kingdom of the world to the kingdom of God is to willingly surrender control of your life. To gain what is eternal, you must let go of everything that is temporary—everything this world cares so much about.

A Christian is any person who turns to Jesus and says, "Everything in my life is negotiable except You." That's what it means to live as a citizen of God's kingdom.

A Christian is any person who turns to Jesus and says, "Everything in my life is negotiable except You."

> *What are the main values and concerns of modern culture?*
>
> *When have you had trouble submitting control over a specific area of your life?*
>
> *When have you been victorious at breaking free from the kingdom of the world?*

ENGAGE

One of the main blessings of studying God's Word as part of a community is that you get the benefit of searching for truth together. As the saying goes, two heads are better than one—and several heads are even better than two. With that in mind, work as a group to compare and contrast the values of God's kingdom with the values of the world's kingdom.

Use the chart below to organize your discussion. What are the main goals or ambitions for each kingdom in connection with the following areas of life:

	Kingdom of God	Kingdom of the World
Marriage		
Parenting		
Friendship		
Work		
Career		
Finances		
Entertainment		

PRAYER REQUESTS

....
....
....
....
....
....
....
....

In addition to studying God's Word, work with your group leader to create a plan for personal study, worship, and application between now and the next session. Select from the following optional activities to match your personal preferences and available time.

⬆ Worship

☑ Read your Bible. Complete the reading plan on page 140.

☐ Spend time with God by engaging the devotional experience on page 141.

☐ Connect with God each day through prayer.

➡ ⬅ Personal Study

☐ Read and interact with "God's Kingdom Is 'Now and Not Yet'" on page 142.

☐ Read and interact with "Christians Live as Citizens of God's Kingdom" on page 144.

⬅ ➡ Application

☐ Be intentional about making the most of your experiences at church this weekend. Take advantage of opportunities to engage other disciples of Jesus in a more meaningful way.

☐ Memorize John 1:29: "The next day John saw Jesus coming toward him and said, 'Here is the Lamb of God, who takes away the sin of the world!'"

☐ When you have an opportunity to participate in Jesus' mission this week, invite another disciple to join you.

☐ Start a journal to record the different ways you engage Jesus' mission for the world each day. This is a great way to remind yourself of that mission and evaluate your participation in it.

☐ Other:

READING PLAN

Read through the following Scripture passages this week. Use the space provided to record your thoughts and responses.

Day 1
Genesis 12:1-9

Day 2
Jeremiah 31:31-40

Day 3
Daniel 2:27-45

Day 4
Matthew 6:19-34

Day 5
John 18:28-40

Day 6
1 Corinthians 15:50-58

Day 7
Revelation 22:1-21

THE MODEL PRAYER

We've seen how Jesus referenced God's will and God's kingdom in the model prayer He used to instruct His disciples. We typically refer to this prayer as the Lord's Prayer, and it has served as a guide to countless numbers of Jesus' followers throughout the centuries.

The version of Jesus' prayer found below is more compact than the one recorded in Matthew 6:9-13, but the vital elements are still there. Read this prayer out loud as an act of worship and obedience. As you do, focus on how the words apply to you specifically as a member of God's kingdom rather than the kingdom of the world.

> [1] He was praying in a certain place, and when he finished, one of his disciples said to him, "Lord, teach us to pray, just as John also taught his disciples."
>
> [2] He said to them, "Whenever you pray, say,
>
> Father,
> your name be honored as holy.
> Your kingdom come.
> [3] Give us each day our daily bread.
> [4] And forgive us our sins,
> for we ourselves also forgive everyone
> in debt to us.
> And do not bring us into temptation."
> LUKE 11:1-4

What emotions and/or memories come to mind when you read through this prayer?

How does this prayer guide your actions and attitudes as a member of God's kingdom?

GOD'S KINGDOM IS "NOW AND NOT YET"

As we've seen, if someone were to ask you the same question the Pharisees asked Jesus in Luke 17—When will the kingdom of God come to earth?—it would be hard for you to give a wrong answer. Throughout the Gospels, Jesus both spoke of God's kingdom as something that "is in your midst" and something that is yet to come. Accordingly, modern theologians have helpfully described God's kingdom as both "now and not yet."

The kingdom of God is already here in the sense that every Christian is a part of that kingdom. Those who follow God have placed their lives under the reign of King Jesus, and every church is an outpost of His kingdom. Yet God's kingdom is also obviously not yet here—not in full, at least. Our world is marked by pain, brokenness, wickedness, and death. It bears all the marks of still awaiting the rightful King's ascent to the throne.

Some day, King Jesus will return to finally conquer all His enemies and set up an eternal and perfect kingdom. While His kingdom is among us, that day is yet to come.

> *How has the presence of God's kingdom on earth benefited those who are not part of that kingdom?*

> *In what ways have you felt the tension of living in the world as a member of God's kingdom?*

This theme of "now and not yet" continues in the New Testament as we move beyond the Gospels:

> [17] Instruct those who are rich in the present age not to be arrogant or to set their hope on the uncertainty of wealth, but on God, who richly provides us with all things to enjoy. [18] Instruct them to do what is good, to be rich in good works, to be generous and willing to share, [19] storing up treasure for themselves as a good foundation for the coming age, so that they may take hold of what is truly life.
> 1 TIMOTHY 6:17-19

Here again we have two specific periods of time: "the present age" and "the coming age." Paul warned his readers against living as if the present age was all that mattered. Instead, he encouraged them to set their priorities based on the age to come.

Paul offered similar instructions to Titus, another one of his disciples:

> [11] For the grace of God has appeared, bringing salvation for all people, [12] instructing us to deny godlessness and worldly lusts and to live in a sensible, righteous, and godly way in the present age, [13] while we wait for the blessed hope, the appearing of the glory of our great God and Savior, Jesus Christ. [14] He gave himself for us to redeem us from all lawlessness and to cleanse for himself a people for his own possession, eager to do good works.
> TITUS 2:11-14

What are some expectations from these Scripture passages that you can apply in your everyday life?

It's important to remember that our world is currently in a time of transition. When Jesus came to earth in human form (what we call the incarnation), He began the process of moving the world out of the present age and into the age to come. It's been a long process. Two thousand years later, society is still broken—still suffering the pains of the present age—and yet every day God's people join in His work to advance His kingdom further and deeper into the world.

When Jesus returns to the earth, He will complete the process. His return will end the present age and finally establish the age to come in fullness and glory. Until that day comes, however, the world will remain caught in the tension between the "now" and the "not yet." And so will we.

What disciplines and practices will help you live well in the tension between the present age and the age to come?

CHRISTIANS LIVE AS CITIZENS OF GOD'S KINGDOM

To be a Christian is to gladly place every area of your life under the reign of King Jesus—to kneel before Him and say, "Everything in my life is negotiable except You." That's the price of citizenship in the kingdom of God. But what do we gain? What are the benefits of membership in God's kingdom?

The apostle John gave us a glimpse of what it means to enjoy life in the kingdom of God.

¹ Then I saw a new heaven and a new earth; for the first heaven and the first earth had passed away, and the sea was no more. ² I also saw the holy city, the new Jerusalem, coming down out of heaven from God, prepared like a bride adorned for her husband.

³ Then I heard a loud voice from the throne:

Look, God's dwelling is with humanity,
and he will live with them.
They will be his peoples,
and God himself will be with them
and will be their God.
⁴ He will wipe away every tear from their eyes.
Death will be no more;
grief, crying, and pain will be no more,
because the previous things have passed away.
REVELATION 21:1-4

What emotions do you experience when you read these verses?

John was describing heaven, of course. God gave him a vision, a glimpse, of what life will be like when God's will is fully accomplished throughout the universe—when His kingdom comes to earth without rebellion, corruption, or compromise.

This is our future as followers of God and members of His kingdom. This is what we look forward to as we live and minister in this present age of sin.

Until that day comes, however, we have work to do. Being a member of God's kingdom is not a passive experience—at least, it shouldn't be. We are not simply passengers on a cruise-liner called Earth, waiting in comfort until we arrive at our heavenly destination.

Instead, God has called us to give our time, talents, energy, resources, and even our very lives—all for the goal of advancing His kingdom in the world.

> *Read the following passages of Scripture and record what they teach about our responsibilities as earthly members of God's kingdom.*
>
> *Matthew 22:37-40*
>
> *Matthew 28:18-20*
>
> *John 17:20-26*
>
> *Acts 1:4-8*

Of course, there are also immediate benefits to being citizens of God's kingdom. We are blessed with the forgiveness of our sins, for example. We can experience the joy of true community. And we have the unbelievable privilege of connecting with and relating to the Creator of the universe.

Imagine you are speaking with a friend about what it means to be a Christian—a citizen of God's kingdom. How would you answer the following questions?

What are Christians supposed to do?

What are Christians not supposed to do?

THE DOCTRINE OF THE HOLY SPIRIT

The Spirit empowers God's people to live for Jesus.

REFLECT

In the previous session we explored the definition of God's kingdom as a "now and not yet" reality. We saw that God's kingdom is present on earth whenever people are in submission to His will, yet will not become fully manifest in the universe until the day of judgment. Until that occurs, Christians have a responsibility to help advance God's kingdom as citizens.

Before we engage the doctrine of the Holy Spirit, take a few moments to reflect on and discuss your recent experiences.

Which of the assignments did you explore this week? How did it go?

What did you learn or experience while reading the Bible?

What questions would you like to ask?

PRAY

Begin the session by connecting with God through prayer. Use the following guidelines as you speak with Him:

- Thank God that He is at work in your life and in the world.

- Ask Him to speak to you today and open your eyes to how He works through the power of His Spirit.

- Pray that a biblical understanding of the Holy Spirit would be evident and encouraging over the next week of study.

INTRODUCTION

Did you know windmills have been around for centuries? They were first constructed in the region we call Iran today, and they date all the way back to 200 B.C. In recent years, windmills have become a major source of energy throughout the world. We usually refer to these modern creations as turbines, and they work to harness the invisible, weightless, formless, and powerful force of the wind.

Think about that for a moment. You can't see the wind, but you can see its effects. You can't grab the wind, but you can harness its great power. Jesus hinted at this reality during a conversation with a religious leader.

> The wind blows where it pleases, and you hear its sound, but you don't know where it comes from or where it is going. So it is with everyone born of the Spirit.
> JOHN 3:8

Like the wind, the Spirit of God is invisible, weightless, formless—and immeasurably powerful. Indeed, God created the world through the power of the Spirit. Jesus performed miracles, endured the cross, and rose from the dead in the power of the Spirit. And through that same power, God moves in the lives of people to know Him and to serve Him.

People are often confused about the Holy Spirit. Some have chosen to belittle the Spirit because they're skeptical or even uncomfortable about God moving in their lives. Others have abused the teaching of the Holy Spirit, making Him the focal point of their ministry and blaming the Spirit for all kinds of strange behavior. Still others have stayed away from the subject entirely because of theological disagreements.

What have you been taught about the role and work of the Holy Spirit?

In what ways have you experienced the Spirit in your life?

What we need today isn't less of God's Spirit, but more. We don't need to be afraid of the Spirit's power in our lives. Instead, we need more dependence on His power and His support as we seek to follow God.

KNOW THE STORY

Just before Jesus' death, He met with His disciples one last time. The shadow of the cross was looming and Jesus knew soon He would no longer be with them. Gathered around a table to share their last meal together, Jesus spoke words of comfort to His friends. He also spoke about the Spirit of God.

15 If you love me, you will keep my commands. 16 And I will ask the Father, and he will give you another Counselor to be with you forever. 17 He is the Spirit of truth. The world is unable to receive him because it doesn't see him or know him. But you do know him, because he remains with you and will be in you. 18 I will not leave you as orphans; I am coming to you. 19 In a little while the world will no longer see me, but you will see me. Because I live, you will live too.
JOHN 14:15-19

7 Nevertheless, I am telling you the truth. It is for your benefit that I go away, because if I don't go away the Counselor will not come to you. If I go, I will send him to you. 8 When he comes, he will convict the world about sin, righteousness, and judgment: 9 About sin, because they do not believe in me; 10 about righteousness, because I am going to the Father and you will no longer see me; 11 and about judgment, because the ruler of this world has been judged.
JOHN 16:7-11

What do these verses teach us about the Holy Spirit?

What questions would you like to ask about the role of the Spirit in this world?

God wants to be with you. He wants to walk with you throughout your day and never leave you. How is that possible? Because of the Holy Spirit! Through the Spirit, God has provided everything you need to know Him, follow Him, serve Him, love Him, and enjoy Him forever.

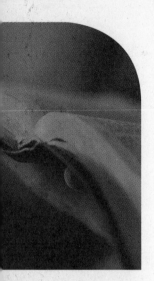

UNPACK THE STORY

WHO IS THE HOLY SPIRIT?

As with the other members of the Trinity, the best way to study the Holy Spirit is to answer two key questions. Here's the first: Who is the Holy Spirit? There are three main ways to answer that question, and all three are necessary for a proper understanding of God's Spirit.

1. The Holy Spirit is a Person. The Holy Spirit isn't a force. He's not energy in the universe or some kind of mystical power. The Holy Spirit is a Person. Jesus referred to the Spirit as "Him" or "He" six times in John 14:15-19. He is a Person. He speaks, prays, testifies, leads, commands, guides, and appoints. He can be grieved, lied to, insulted, or blasphemed. He has thoughts and desires. He makes decisions and has emotions.

How can we relate to the Spirit in a personal way?

> The Holy Spirit isn't a force. He's not energy in the universe or some kind of mystical power. The Holy Spirit is a Person.

2. The Holy Spirit is God. The Holy Spirit is the third Person of the Trinity. Again, the Trinity is a hard concept to grasp—how can the Spirit be a separate Person from the Father and the Son, yet still part of one Being? We don't know for sure. We can't understand the Trinity in full. Still, we can trust what God has revealed in His Word.

3. The Holy Spirit is Truth. The Spirit is the Source of truth, and He guides you into all truth (see John 14:17). Specifically, the Spirit had a vital role in the creation of the Bible.

> [20] Above all, you know this: No prophecy of Scripture comes from the prophet's own interpretation, [21] because no prophecy ever came by the will of man; instead, men spoke from God as they were carried along by the Holy Spirit.
> 2 PETER 1:20-21

The reason you have a Bible is because of the Spirit's work revealing truth in a way you can understand it. But He not only reveals truth, He also leads you into truth. The Spirit points to Jesus who said, "I am the way, the truth, and the life" (John 14:6).

How does the Spirit help us engage the Scriptures today?

WHAT DOES THE SPIRIT DO?

Here's the second question: What does the Holy Spirit do? Let's look at two primary ways the Spirit works in our lives as we follow Christ.

1. The Holy Spirit facilitates salvation. Salvation is a work of the Spirit. Yes, salvation is centered on faith in Jesus Christ, but we need to understand that no one can be saved or come to know Jesus apart from the Spirit's work in his or her life. The Holy Spirit convicts us of our sin, points us to Christ, and reveals the truth of Jesus. It's through the Spirit that we pass from death to life in that wonderful moment we refer to as "being saved."

Look back at John 16:7-11. How have you seen these works of the Spirit on a large scale?

Looking at your own life, how did the Holy Spirit convict you of your sin and draw you to Jesus?

2. The Spirit produces transformation. Not only does the Holy Spirit facilitate your salvation, but He also transforms you to become more and more like Jesus. God loves you too much to leave you the way you are. His goal is to make you into a new person who reflects both the character and the priorities of Jesus.

Consider this quote from author Bill Bright:

> "The Spirit-filled Christian has given up his own powerless, defeated and fruitless life for the supernatural power, victory and fruitfulness of Jesus Christ. This is what we mean by the supernatural life. When a Christian is living supernaturally, he is filled with the Holy Spirit—filled with Jesus Christ, allowing God to work in him and through him."[1]

God loves you too much to leave you the way you are. His goal is to make you into a new person who reflects both the character and the priorities of Jesus.

What steps can we take to more fully experience the Spirit's presence and power each day?

ENGAGE

Use the last part of your time together by splitting up into smaller groups and discussing more personal applications concerning the power of the Holy Spirit in your lives. Allow yourself to be open and honest about the following discussion points.

Discussion Point 1: We studied how the Spirit of God transforms our lives by promising to change us, lead us, and empower us. Share with your group an area where you need the Spirit to work in your life. For example, maybe you need Him to break a sinful habit, change an attitude, lead you in a decision, give you boldness, or empower you to serve God more fully. Talk these things through and pray for one another.

Discussion Point 2: Discuss what you've learned and how to put it into practice. The Spirit is always leading us to take action. In fact, the Book of Acts is really about the action of the Holy Spirit in the early church. Everywhere you turn in that book, the Spirit of God is moving! He is leading, directing, prompting, empowering, opening doors of opportunity and doing miraculous things. Discuss with your group what the Spirit of God is leading you to do. If you're not sure what that is yet, pray as a group for the Spirit to reveal to you what actions He wants you to take. Ask Him for boldness as you follow His lead.

PRAYER REQUESTS

....

....

....

....

....

....

....

....

....

....

1. Bill Bright, *The Holy Spirit: The Key to Supernatural Living,* Campus Crusade, 1980, 59.

WEEKLY ACTIVITIES

In addition to studying God's Word, work with your group leader to create a plan for personal study, worship, and application between now and the next session. Select from the following optional activities to match your personal preferences and available time.

⬆ Worship

☑ Read your Bible. Complete the reading plan on page 154.

☐ Spend time with God by engaging the devotional experience on page 155.

☐ The Spirit empowers us to worship God in special ways. Take a moment to look up these central verses on how the Spirit empowers biblical, God-honoring worship: Ephesians 5:18-21; 6:18; 1 Corinthians 12:1-11; and Romans 5:5.

➡⬅ Personal Study

☐ Read and interact with "Who Is the Holy Spirit?" on page 156.

☐ Read and interact with "What Does the Holy Spirit Do?" on page 158.

⬅➡ Application

☐ At the end of your group time, you discussed how the Holy Spirit is leading you to action. If you don't yet know how the Holy Spirit is leading you, spend time in prayer for the Spirit to reveal to you what actions He wants you to take. Then ask Him for boldness as you follow His lead.

☐ Memorize Galatians 5:16: "I say then, walk by the Spirit and you will certainly not carry out the desire of the flesh."

☐ Journal about your life in regard to the Spirit. Galatians 5 describes the life that is under the control of the Spirit. Take time to read Galatians 5:22-23. Identify the character qualities that the Spirit produces in a person's life. Then journal a prayer for the areas you would like to see more of in your own life.

☐ Other:

WORSHIP

READING PLAN

Read through the following Scripture passages this week. Use the space provided to record your thoughts and responses.

Day 1
John 16:7-15

Day 2
Acts 1:1-8

Day 3
John 14:25-31

Day 4
Romans 8:26-28

Day 5
Isaiah 11:2

Day 6
John 14:12-17

Day 7
Ezekiel 36:25-28

JESUS AND THE HOLY SPIRIT

Jesus' power was always attributed to the power of the Spirit. Look at some of the following examples from the New Testament:

- The Spirit was involved in the birth of Christ. According to Matthew 1:18, before Mary and Joseph were married, she was found to be pregnant by the Holy Spirit.
- In another account, an angel appeared to Mary and declared that she would bear the Messiah. She said, "How can this be, since I have not had sexual relations with a man?" The angel said, "The Holy Spirit will come upon you, and the power of the Most High will overshadow you. Therefore, the holy one to be born will be called the Son of God" (Luke 1:34-35).
- The Spirit was also involved in the growth and development of Jesus. In Luke 2:40, Jesus "grew up and became strong, filled with wisdom, and God's grace was on him."
- At His baptism, Jesus was anointed by the Holy Spirit and launched His public ministry (see Matt. 3:13-17).
- Jesus was led by the Spirit into the wilderness to be tempted and came out empowered by the Spirit (see Luke 4:1-14).
- In His first sermon, Luke 4:18, He said, "The Spirit of the Lord is on me."
- It was by the power of the Spirit that He drove out demons, taught the multitude, and gave Him joy in ministry.
- Hebrews 9:14 says that by the Spirit Jesus offered Himself up to God as a sacrifice, and Romans 8:11 says that by that same Spirit Jesus was raised from the dead.

From beginning to end, Jesus was led and empowered by the Holy Spirit. That was the secret to His ministry! While Jesus was fully God, He was also fully man. And the same power Jesus held—power that came directly from His dependence on the Holy Spirit—is available to you and me. The Spirit wants to move powerfully in your life, but your access to the Spirit's power is in direct relationship to your dependence on Him. Greater dependence on the Spirit, greater power. Little dependence, little power.

How are you experiencing the Spirit's power in your life today?

You can live just like Jesus. First John 2:6 says, "The one who says he remains in him should walk just as he walked." You can walk as Jesus walked, live as He lived, serve as He served, and love as He loved. But you can't do that in your own strength. You can only do it as you rely every day on the power of God's Spirit in your life.

PERSONAL STUDY

WHO IS THE HOLY SPIRIT?

The Holy Spirit is a Person. Long before Jesus came to earth, God's people were struggling. Worship was dry. Sins were weighing them down. There was little change in their lives. They were frustrated in the little progress they had made spiritually. God promised them that one day He would give them a new heart and a new Spirit to live within them. He spoke these words through the prophet Ezekiel:

> I will give you a new heart and put a new spirit within you; I will remove your heart of stone and give you a heart of flesh.
> EZEKIEL 36:26

This promise came true when Jesus sent the Holy Spirit to His disciples. Jesus knew that His disciples were going to be devastated after His crucifixion. He knew they would feel abandoned and alone, so He said He was going to send "another helper"—a Person just like Him who would be with them forever, meet their every need, and never leave them.

Just after Jesus' death and resurrection, He instructed His disciples to go back to Jerusalem and wait for the Spirit to come. Then, on the Jewish holiday called Pentecost, the Spirit began to move powerfully on them. They were filled with boldness to preach the gospel. More than 3,000 people were saved that day and the church began (see Acts 2). Ever since that day, God has been moving in the hearts of His people through the power of His Spirit.

How have you experienced frustration in your relationship with God?

What obstacles keep you from relying on the power of God's Spirit?

Jesus said the Spirit of God was our "Advocate" (John 14:26, NIV). Other translations use different terms, including "Counselor" and "Comforter" (KJV). The original Greek word literally means "someone to come alongside."

The Holy Spirit is the Person called to come alongside you. Probably the best translation is simply "Helper" (NASB). The Spirit will be with you forever and will meet your every need and never leave you, just like He was with the disciples.

The Holy Spirit is God. He is described in many ways throughout the Bible. In Genesis 1:2, He is called "the Spirit of God." In Isaiah 61:1, "The Spirit of the Lord GOD." In Zechariah 12:10, He is the "spirit of grace." David called Him the "Holy Spirit" in Psalm 51:11. In Matthew 10:20, Jesus called Him "the Spirit of your Father." In Romans 1:4, He is called the "Spirit of holiness." In Romans 8:9, He is the "Spirit of Christ." In Galatians 4:6, He is called the "Spirit of his Son." In 1 Peter 4:14, He is the "Spirit of glory." Hebrews 9:14 says He is "the eternal Spirit."

All throughout Scripture we see that the Holy Spirit is God. To follow the Spirit is to follow God. To know the Spirit is to know God. To listen to the Spirit is to listen to God. In fact, all throughout the Scripture, the Holy Spirit possesses the attributes of God:

He is eternal:

> And I will ask the Father, and he will give you another Counselor to be with you forever.
> JOHN 14:16

He is all-knowing:

> Now God has revealed these things to us by the Spirit, since the Spirit searches everything, even the depths of God.
> 1 CORINTHIANS 2:10

He is all-powerful:

> So he answered me, "This is the word of the LORD to Zerubbabel: 'Not by strength or by might, but by my Spirit,' says the LORD of Armies.
> ZECHARIAH 4:6

He is ever-present:

> Where can I go to escape your Spirit? Where can I flee from your presence?
> PSALM 139:7

What else have you learned about the Spirit from your study of Scripture?

PERSONAL STUDY 2

WHAT DOES THE HOLY SPIRIT DO?

The Spirit's work in salvation: The Spirit of God is actively at work when we come to saving faith in Jesus. He convicts us of our sin, points us to Christ, and reveals the truth of Jesus. He also, at the point of our salvation, enables us to call on Jesus to be saved. He washes us, cleans us, makes us a part of God's family, and eternally secures us in Jesus forever! When we choose to follow Jesus, the Spirit indwells us and is with us forever. Just think about it.

You will never be left alone. You will never be apart from God. You will never be separated from God's Spirit.

Let's dig into God's Word and find out what the Spirit does to bring us to salvation. Answer the following questions according to the attached passage.

What does Jesus say the Spirit reveals to us (John 16:13)?

What does the Spirit bring into our hearts (John 16:8)?

What does the Spirit enable you to do (1 Cor. 12:1-11)?

What does the Spirit do for you (Titus 3:5-7)?

How does the Spirit secure you (Eph. 1:13-14)?

Where does the Spirit dwell (1 Cor. 6:19-20)?

The Spirit's work in transformation: From the moment of your spiritual birth, you enter into a new relationship with God, and this new relationship is accomplished by the Holy Spirit. He is the one who convicts you, draws you in, gives you new life, and places you into God's family. But He's also the One who transforms you. Look at some of the following ways the Spirit works after salvation.

The Spirit of God changes you.

> *Read Romans 8:5-8. What are some evidences that the Spirit of God is in control in your life?*

The Spirit of God leads you.

> *Read Romans 8:12-17. Through what specific circumstances have you seen the Spirit lead you?*

The Spirit of God empowers you.

> *Read Acts 1:8 and 1 Corinthians 12:4-7. In what areas do you feel inadequate to be used by God?*

> *How do these passages encourage you in that you are empowered by the Spirit?*

He is the one who convicts you, draws you in, gives you new life, and places you into God's family. He is also the one who changes you from the inside out, making you more and more like Jesus. He leads you in daily decisions, He guides you in wisdom, He convicts and changes parts of your character, and He produces new desires for God and for good. He also fills you with joy, peace, love, kindness, faithfulness, goodness, patience, gentleness, and self-control. It's the Spirit that empowers you to serve God, love others, and share what Jesus has done for you! You cannot accomplish this on your own; it's a work of the Spirit. And the joyful Christian life is a life lived walking in step with the Spirit.

THE DOCTRINE OF THE CHURCH

God's people gather for community
and scatter for a cause.

REFLECT

In the previous session we learned about the Person and the power of the Holy Spirit. The Spirit is active in our salvation and also in our personal transformation. We also learned that the Spirit moved powerfully in the early church, empowering them to boldly preach about Jesus and make disciples.

We'll conclude this exploration of key doctrines by taking a closer look at the church. First, take a moment to talk as a group about your recent experiences.

Which of the assignments did you explore this week? How did it go?

What did you learn or experience while reading the Bible?

What questions would you like to ask?

PRAY

Begin the session by approaching God through prayer. Use the following guidelines as you connect with Him:

- Pray for God's Spirit to move in your time today.

- Pray for your hearts and minds to be open to what God is doing through His church.

- Ask for wisdom as you study what it means to join the church in working to achieve Christ's mission.

INTRODUCTION

Picture the following scenes:

- A small group meets in secret, quietly huddling in a subdued living room. Their presence isn't legal in Saudi Arabia. If they're caught, some could be sent to prison, others could lose their lives. The room falls silent as they hear footsteps outside the door.

- Thousands of affluent suburbanites gather in a large, state-of-the-art building in Atlanta. The lights, video, and production represent the best of the best. People come dressed in casual clothes, carrying their coffee into the worship center. The band cranks up and the room is flooded with moving lights and haze. The people begin to worship with their hands and voices raised.

- Everyone wears white jumpsuits. Guards are posted around the room. As men file in, smiles break across their faces. A band begins to play upbeat music, which fills the hopeless space with joy. The men clap their hands in celebration. A man comes to the microphone and declares: "Brothers, we once were free on the outside. Now we may be in prison, but we are free on the inside!"

- An organ plays as robed choir members sway back and forth to the music. Even though they are few, they make a joyful noise. The people are sitting in old pews, meeting behind stained-glass windows that picture the life of Jesus. The pastor gets up to proclaim hope to his congregation. Outside, the drug dealers and gangs make inner city Detroit a fearful place to live.

- Only one light bulb illuminates the cinder-block building. People rode in the back of pickup trucks for several miles to get there, traversing the jungles of Guatemala. Most hadn't eaten all day, but after the service is over they will share tortillas and soft drinks. Someone stands with a guitar and begins to lead out in song.

What do all these scenes have in common?

What comes to mind when you hear the word "church"?

KNOW THE STORY

The early church was a powerful movement that was both initiated and sustained by God. People were saved. Lives were transformed. The gospel was preached, and people were sent out to tell the nations about Jesus.

Yet even in the early church, there were times when Christians needed a reminder to continue meeting and fulfilling their purpose.

In this passage below, the author of Hebrews reminded his fellow Christians about the wonderful access they have to God because of Jesus. He encouraged them to continue gathering together as a church to fulfill their mission.

> 19 Therefore, brothers and sisters, since we have boldness to enter the sanctuary through the blood of Jesus— 20 he has inaugurated for us a new and living way through the curtain (that is, through his flesh)— 21 and since we have a great high priest over the house of God, 22 let us draw near with a true heart in full assurance of faith, with our hearts sprinkled clean from an evil conscience and our bodies washed in pure water. 23 Let us hold on to the confession of our hope without wavering, since he who promised is faithful. 24 And let us watch out for one another to provoke love and good works, 25 not neglecting to gather together, as some are in the habit of doing, but encouraging each other, and all the more as you see the day approaching.
> HEBREWS 10:19-25

What are your initial reactions to this passage?

On a practical level, what does it mean to "watch out for one another to provoke love and good works"?

As we continue exploring the doctrine of the church, we'll see how this passage not only guides us in understanding what the church is, but also how we should live and work as members of that institution.

UNPACK THE STORY

WHAT IS THE CHURCH?

The church is a family. The church isn't an organization, a business, or an entrepreneurial enterprise. When a person comes to faith in Jesus, he or she becomes part of God's family—the church. Just as someone is born into their physical family, Jesus said you must be "born again" (John 3:3) to get into God's family. In God's family, God is our "Father" (Gal. 4:6), Jesus is our big brother (see Heb. 2:11), and Christians become brothers and sisters (see 1 Cor. 7:15) as members of God's household (see Gal. 6:10).

Earthly families grow when children leave home to start their own families. You don't stop being a member of your family when you leave home, but you do gain the opportunity to expand that family by starting something new. The same is true in the church.

How have you experienced the blessings of a church family?

In God's family, God is our Father, Jesus is our big brother, and Christians become brothers and sisters as members of God's household.

The scenarios you read in the introduction were all diverse pictures of local churches meeting in different places, cultures, and environments. Such meetings are vital for every follower of Christ. It's not enough to be a part of God's family on a grand scale—what we refer to as the "universal church." We also need to be connected to a local collection of disciples.

In other words, God wants you to find a home in a local church family. Scripture confirms this truth. The majority of instruction in the Bible concerning the church has in mind a local congregation of believers. In fact, it would be a foreign concept to the biblical authors to think about being in the universal church without attending a local church.

So, what is the church? Here's one of many possible definitions: *The church is a family of baptized believers in Jesus Christ who gather for community and scatter for the cause of telling the world about Jesus.*

What are the consequences of avoiding membership in a local church?

What would you add to the above definition of "the church"?

GATHER FOR COMMUNITY AND SCATTER FOR A CAUSE

Now that we have a basic definition of the church, let's look at what it means to gather for community and scatter for a cause.

First, God's people are called to be part of a community. The early church experienced community in a way that created inseparable and unbreakable bonds. God worked in powerful ways. The apostles taught, lives were changed, and the Spirit moved. People generously gave to meet one another's needs. They spent their time eating together in their homes and gathering in the temple courts for worship.

It was an incredible period for the church.

Read Acts 2:41-47. What do you find most appealing in these verses? Why?

What obstacles prevent modern churches from experiencing that level of community?

The church isn't only called to gather for community, but also to scatter for a cause. As disciples of Jesus Christ, we are called to make disciples of Jesus Christ—who make disciples, who make more disciples, and so on. That was one of Jesus' final commands.

> ¹⁹ Go, therefore, and make disciples of all nations, baptizing them in the name of the Father and of the Son and of the Holy Spirit, ²⁰ teaching them to observe everything I have commanded you. And remember, I am with you always, to the end of the age.
> MATTHEW 28:19-20

How does the church make it easier for you to spread the gospel in your community?

What hinders the church from having a greater influence in modern culture?

God's people are called to be part of a community. The early church experienced community in a way that created inseparable and unbreakable bonds. God worked in powerful ways.

ENGAGE

We've learned that the church has two primary functions: (1) to gather for community, and (2) to scatter with a cause. It's easy to look at the church described in the Bible and desire to be in a church like that. It seems so perfect, without any problems or challenges. But even the early church was imperfect. They dealt with conflict, baggage from the past, power plays, immorality, and bad leadership. But through it all, people loved Jesus and worked hard to correct the problems and be a true reflection of Jesus to the world.

Today, there are no perfect churches. Churches are filled with and led by imperfect people. And just as there are no perfect families, there are some families that are healthy because they work through conflict, exercise grace and forgiveness, and work together for a common goal. The same is true of the church. When people in churches work through their conflict in the proper way, treat each other with grace and forgiveness, and work together for the sake of the gospel, they find health and peace.

Take a moment to share your church experience in your group.

How can a church practically work through conflict, exercise grace and forgiveness, and work together for a common goal?

PRAYER REQUESTS

....

....

....

....

....

....

....

....

....

In addition to studying God's Word, work with your group leader to create a plan for personal study, worship, and application between now and the next session. Select from the following optional activities to match your personal preferences and available time.

⬆ Worship

☑ Read your Bible. Complete the reading plan on page 168.

☐ Spend time with God by engaging the devotional experience on page 169.

☐ One unique trait of the church is that it gathers to worship Jesus. Sometimes that worship takes place through music, the Lord's Supper, baptism, the reading and teaching of God's Word, giving, and serving. How is the gospel clearly seen as the church worships in each of these ways? Take time this week to worship God with other believers in a local church.

➡ ⬅ Personal Study

☐ Read and interact with "God's People Gather for Community" on page 170.

☐ Read and interact with "God's People Scatter for a Cause" on page 172.

⬅ ➡ Application

☐ Read Hebrews 13:7,17. According to these verses, how should you respond to leaders who seek to lead the church to fulfill the mission of making disciples? Send an email this week to a pastor or church leader who has influenced you the most. Thank them for their example, their faithfulness to teach God's Word, and their investment in your life.

☐ Memorize Hebrews 10:25 (NLT): "Let us not neglect our meeting together, as some people do, but encourage one another, especially now that the day of his return is drawing near."

☐ Journal your church experience. Take some time to get alone with God and reflect on your church experience. You may have had a wonderful church experience or perhaps one that has been hurtful or disappointing. Write down your reflections in a letter to God. Ask Him to remove any pain inflicted by people in the church and to replace it with a love for His church.

☐ Other:

 **WORSHIP**

READING PLAN

Read through the following Scripture passages this week. Use the space provided to record your thoughts and responses.

Day 1
Colossians 3:12-17

Day 2
Acts 2:37-47

Day 3
Ephesians 2:13-22

Day 4
Romans 12:4-8

Day 5
Ephesians 4:1-16

Day 6
1 Corinthians 16:10-24

Day 7
Romans 16:17-20

THE BRIDE OF CHRIST

Jesus loves His church. In fact, the church is called the "bride of Christ." In Ephesians 5:25-27, the apostle Paul describes the kind of love Jesus has for His church. He said that Jesus loved the church so much that He "gave himself for her." This is a reference to the cross. Jesus loved His church and His people so much that He was willing to endure whatever sacrifice, pay whatever price needed to restore them back to fellowship with Him.

Picture how much a young groom loves his bride. He watches her walk down the aisle, her white dress trailing behind her, her face aglow with love for her husband. The ring of his affection glistens from her finger, a symbol of his covenant love for her. He has chosen her. He has sacrificed for her. He is committed to protecting, leading, and loving her for the rest of his life. He has a home prepared for her, and soon he will gather her in his arms and carry her across that threshold, and his love for her will never die. That is a picture of how Jesus feels about you—His church, His bride. Jesus has set His affection and love on you. He has bought you with His own blood through His sacrifice on the cross (see 1 Pet. 1:18-19). He has made a covenant, an eternal promise that He will never break (see Matt. 26:28). He has made you clean, washing away your sin and making you right with Him (see 1 John 1:9), and one day He is coming to get you.

Revelation 19:6-7 describes the end of time. Jesus will come for His bride! He will gather His church up in His arms and take us to His Father's house in heaven where we will be with Him forever (see John 14:2-3). That's how much Jesus loves His church. That's how much Jesus loves you.

> **What emotions do you experience when you think about Christ's love for the church? What stands out to you most about His love for us?**

Paul says Jesus also loved the church enough to purify and clean up His church. When you become a part of God's family, Jesus not only restores you back to Himself, but He cleans you up, inside and out. All the old life, the old mistakes, the old baggage is gone and you are pure and clean in His eyes. Jesus also loves His church so much that He promises to never leave His church. God has no orphans. He never leaves His people. He will never forsake you. You are His forever.

GOD'S PEOPLE GATHER FOR COMMUNITY

The church is a group of believers who gather to experience biblical community. Acts 2:42-47 gives us a great snapshot of what this biblical community looks like.

> [42] They devoted themselves to the apostles' teaching, to the fellowship, to the breaking of bread, and to prayer. [43] Everyone was filled with awe, and many wonders and signs were being performed through the apostles. [44] Now all the believers were together and held all things in common. [45] They sold their possessions and property and distributed the proceeds to all, as any had need. [46] Every day they devoted themselves to meeting together in the temple, and broke bread from house to house. They ate their food with joyful and sincere hearts, [47] praising God and enjoying the favor of all the people. Every day the Lord added to their number those who were being saved.
> ACTS 2:42-47

Let's look at the four key elements of biblical community given to us in verse 42.

The church devoted themselves to the apostle's teaching. One key element of a biblical church is devotion to the preaching and teaching of God's Word. This was the very thing Paul was referring to when he said, "And now I commit you to God and to the word of his grace, which is able to build you up and to give you an inheritance among all who are sanctified" (Acts 20:32).

How have you seen growth in the church because of a commitment to the teaching and preaching of God's Word?

What did Paul mean when he wrote a commitment to the Word "is able to build you up and to give you an inheritance among all who are sanctified"?

The church devoted themselves to fellowship. Not only were they devoted to God's Word, they were devoted to each other. The word *fellowship* means to be partners together. It means to share life together. Far from just coming to church and quickly leaving, fellowship means spending time caring for each other and partnering together in the gospel.

What would you consider genuine Christian fellowship?

The church devoted themselves to breaking bread. Some interpret this to mean simply sharing meals together, and the early church certainly did that. Acts 2:46 says: "Every day they devoted themselves to meeting together in the temple, and broke bread from house to house. They ate their food with joyful and sincere hearts." But the breaking of bread in Acts 2:42 could also refer to the Lord's Supper, a special meal observed by Christ followers to remember the death, burial, and resurrection of Jesus.

Why is it important for believers to be reminded of the gospel of Christ by partaking in the Lord's Supper together?

What are other ways the church can be intentional about reminding each other of Christ's sacrifice on the cross?

The church devoted themselves to prayers. The early church was a praying church. There are times when we need to pray alone (see Matt. 6:6), but there are also times when it's important for the church to gather together and pray for each other.

Which of these elements of biblical community is carried out best in your church? What makes it so effective?

How can you contribute to one of these elements in the life of your church?

GOD'S PEOPLE SCATTER FOR A CAUSE

The early church took Jesus' mandate to tell the world seriously. Within two years, they had "filled Jerusalem" with the gospel (Acts 5:28). Within five years there were multiple churches (Acts 9:31). In 19 years, they had "turned the world upside down" (Acts 17:6), and within 28 years, the gospel had spread all over the known world (see Col. 1:5-6).

Which is most impressive to you?

Why do you think the early church had so much success with the spreading of the gospel?

The early church took Jesus' mandate in the Great Commission seriously, and the church today still takes seriously the Great Commission to tell the world the hope we have in Jesus. That is why men and women, college students, families, vocational missionaries, and volunteer workers go all around the world to declare the good news of the gospel.

Sharing with people the message of life is the job of the church. We are "ambassadors for Christ" (2 Cor. 5:20-21). Just as an ambassador lives in a foreign land, we are strangers and foreigners in this world, and our citizenship is in heaven. While we live in this world, we reflect Christ to people who don't know Him, and we tell people the good news about Jesus. Telling people about Jesus is a huge privilege for the church, but it's also an awesome responsibility.

Who shared the gospel with you for the first time?

Why do you think it's important for the church to be actively sharing the gospel?

The apostle Paul said he was "obligated" to take the gospel to every kind of people (see Rom. 1:14). He boldly proclaimed the gospel because it is "the power of God for salvation to everyone who believes" (Rom. 1:16). God still changes people's lives today when they hear the gospel and believe on Jesus for their salvation. Paul also wrote this in 2 Timothy:

> What you have heard from me in the presence of many witnesses, commit to faithful men who will be able to teach others also.
> 2 TIMOTHY 2:2

What was Paul telling Timothy in this passage? How is this applicable for us today?

Read the following passages, and record how each speaks to the spreading of the gospel. Then comment on how we can apply each to our own ministry to the world.

1 Thessalonians 1:6-8

1 Timothy 2:3-4

Revelation 7:9

What are practical ways churches can do a better job at scattering for a cause? Give several examples.

REFLECT AND CONNECT

Finish Volume 2 with a time of review
and fellowship as a group.

REFLECT

The previous session concluded our brief exploration of the basic doctrines of the Christian faith. We saw that the doctrine of the church encourages members of God's kingdom to gather for community and then scatter to make an impact in the world.

Which of the assignments did you explore this week? How did it go?

What did you learn or experience while reading the Bible?

What questions would you like to ask?

As we conclude Volume 2 of *Disciples Path: The Journey,* use this final session as an opportunity to review what you've learned and enjoy spending time together as a community. When helpful, use the following questions to help guide your conversations.

What have you recently learned or explored more deeply about your identity as a disciple of Jesus?

What have you liked best about digging into Bible doctrine? Why?

What's a "next step" you are currently pursuing as a disciple of Christ?

PRAY

Conclude this session with an extended time of prayer as a group. Allow each member an opportunity to share both praises and requests for intercession. Conclude by praying together in whatever method is most comfortable and productive.

TAKE THE NEXT STEP OF YOUR JOURNEY.

Congratulations on completing Volume 2 of *The Journey*. Use the momentum you've established with Volumes 1 and 2 by continuing with Volume 3, which dives deeply into the life of a disciple. The material explores the vital disciplines of reading the Bible, prayer, living in community, and relying on the Holy Spirit. It also places a heavy emphasis on evangelism and mission.

disciplespath.com/thejourney
Order online or call 800.458.2772